You can't have your kayak and heat it

FRANK MUIR & DENIS NORDEN

YOU CAN'T HAVE YOUR KAYAK AND HEAT IT

Stories from

MY WORD!

with an introduction by Sir Jack Longland

EYRE
METHUEN

First published in 1973
by Eyre Methuen Ltd
11 New Fetter Lane, London EC4P 4EE
© *1973 by Frank Muir and Denis Norden*
Introduction © *1973 by Sir Jack Longland*
Printed in Great Britain
by Butler & Tanner Ltd
Frome and London

ISBN 0 413 30660 7

CONTENTS

INTRODUCTION

I WAS a devotee of Frank Muir and Denis Norden's *Take It From Here* long before Tony Shryane and Ted Mason invented *My Word!* and so gave me the chance to meet the two great, or at any rate very tall men in person. There, I've done it again. The trouble about long acquaintanceship with Frank and Denis is that you start trying to imitate them, and all it comes out as, is Frank taken with a lot of water, or Denis without the vitriol.

This book is a collection of what *My Word!* listeners usually refer to as 'those stories at the end'. Now in its sixteenth year, *My Word!* is probably the most widely-heard radio show in the world. The major part of the programme is a quiz on words and quotations, during which Frank and Denis are most splendidly partnered by Dilys Powell and Anne Scott-James. However, for the last round, I give Frank and Denis a quotation each. I then ask each of them to relate his own unlikely version of how that quotation came into use. The resulting exercises in imagination have, over the years, produced a form of language-surgery they have made uniquely their own.

The title of this book is a fair example of what desperation can lend to invention. It is taken from an early programme, where the quotation I offered was 'you can't have your cake and eat it'. In return, I was told a cautionary tale of a slow-witted Eskimo. In an endeavour to keep his feet warm while afloat, he kindled a small fire amidships and kept it going by breaking off more and more pieces of his frail craft. It was only as the icy waters closed over his head that the moral of this book's title was borne in upon him.

The discerning reader will not need the identifying frieze at the head of each story to tell him, as in the Catechism, which is M. and which is N. I know, of course, some of the legends of their sustained partnership as scriptwriters, both lolling in a room too small for them, with their long legs propped on the table in the middle, whilst the script emerged in one piece, as from some mysterious intellectual ticker-tape machine. At all events, their script-writing jointmanship was so renowned that, when each began separately to invent his own *My Word!* stories, I expected that the results would be almost identical.

In fact, as BBC listeners know, the success of *My Word!* is due to Denis's stories being completely different, in method, character and tone, from those spun by Frank. And yet the two story-styles complement each other, as do the personalities of their authors, so that the programme often does emerge as a single work of art, jointly composed by two hands.

In these stories Frank Muir is the more flamboyant, extrovert, never missing a chance of playing a character; he inhabits a zany world in which he, or you, will suffer the most humiliating and self-inflicted catastrophes – but yet a less sinister world than that in which Denis Norden knows, before he begins, that he is the chosen enemy of the Fates. Denis is a metropolitan character, city-anchored. He is more likely to write of runaway Hors d'œuvres trolleys than of runaway horses. His comments on the world as he finds it, and as it finds him, are quietly but savagely incisive. Frank is the supreme exponent of the dotty juxtaposition of the doubly or trebly incongruous, but each instance has its own insane logic, usually backed by an impeccably accurate historical reference.

Your turn now, and I needn't wish you good luck. 'Here is God's plenty.'

JACK LONGLAND

Mad, bad, and dangerous to know

Lady Caroline Lamb
of Byron, in her Journal

NOW that I am in my fifties, and looking forward to the first glimmerings of the approach of the beginning of the first foothills of early middle-age, I can look back, in my tweedy, pipe-smoking way, to the searingly painful process of growing up and be glad that it is at last almost over.

I suppose my most traumatic period was when I was fourteen. A lot of significant things happened to me that year: my nickname was changed from 'Flossie' to 'Raker', I became aware of my personal appearance, and I discovered Women – or, to be more precise, Maudie Thwaites.

Up until this hinge in my life I had been a happy enough little lad. We lived at Broadstairs and I enjoyed a healthy, open-air life, losing one sandal every day on the beach and riding my bike; I had one of the first dynamos, a great thing the size of a teapot which clamped to the front wheel with such force that I had to stand on the pedals to get the bike to go faster than 2 m.p.h. And I was a short, chubby fellow, addicted to candy-floss – hence my nickname, Flossie.

On or about my fourteenth birthday a number of dramatic changes occurred. Almost overnight I shot up from being five foot one and a half inches to being six foot three inches, and my teeth started to splay out – hence my new nickname of The Rake, or Raker. Bets were laid at my school on whether I could eat an apple through a tennis racquet.

And I fell madly in love with Maudie Thwaites. With the wisdom of hindsight I can't think why I did this, apart from the undeniable truth that she was there. She was very short indeed, and dumpy with it. She wore spectacles, which she was in the habit of pushing back up her nose with a forefinger about every third second, and she preferred sniffing to having a good blow. And she always seemed to be leaning up against a wall. She would spend whole evenings leaning up against a wall, pushing her spectacles back up and sniffing. I don't think I have ever met anybody since, with the possible exception of the late Mr Maurice Winnick, so devoted to leaning up against a wall. She also kept saying 'I'm bored'.

It was a period of the most acute agony for me. I had become extremely self-conscious about my appearance, which meant that I was overcome with shyness if anybody even looked in my direction, let alone spoke to me.

I tried to improve my appearance. I went at my hair with fistfuls of solidified brilliantine. To make myself look spotty like the older boys I stuck little round bits of cut-up inner-tube on my chin and neck with fish glue. I persuaded my parents to let me have a brace on my teeth – a device made of gold wire which went round the front of the teeth with two little screws at the back which, when tightened a quarter of a turn every other day, dragged the teeth, squealing, back into the skull. But all to little avail.

Whenever I joined Maud at a wall, all six foot three of me, with my rubber spots and my hair sticking out like a sweep's brush dipped in sump oil, she would just sniff and say 'I'm bored'. And I couldn't think of anything to say back.

This was partly because I didn't know what 'bored' meant. It wasn't a word which had crossed my path before. I thought it meant something like 'I'm Belgian'. So I would just lean with her in miserable silence for an hour or so and go home. What, I asked myself desperately, does one DO with a woman?

The whole affair might have ended there had not a friend lent me a book. I was quite interested in moths and butterflies at the time and when my friend slipped this book to me and whispered its name in class I accepted it gratefully; I thought he had whispered 'Lady Chatterley's Larva'. On the way home in the tram I started reading it and it wasn't about larva at all. It was about a gamekeeper and a lady in a wood and he was chewing her ear. But what interested me was that the lady liked it. It had never occurred to me that what ladies wanted was not being talked to but something much easier to do – having an ear chewed.

Elated, I sought out Maud and found her leaning up against the Public Library wall.

'I'm bored,' she said.

With quiet confidence I leaned down and gave her ear a thorough gnawing.

Now one thing I omitted to mention was that Maud was an ear-ring girl. Some girls are ear-ring girls and some are celluloid slide girls and some are slave-bangle girls. But Maud was an ear-ring girl and that night she was sporting a large, complicated pair made of bent wire in the shape of gladioli.

And as I tried to straighten up – my back was beginning to give – I found that I couldn't. It was as though we were welded together. A moment's panic, a brief exploration, and the ghastly truth was apparent: her ear-ring and my tooth-brace had somehow got twisted round each other and we were fast-lodged.

It was during the ensuing two hours, before we got to Margate General Hospital and the Casualty Officer disconnected us, that I left childish things behind me and became a man. My emergence from the chrysalis was somewhat accelerated by the language Maud used; a string of words entirely new to me – I tried one out on my mother when I got home and she caught me such a cracker with her ring-finger hand that I ricocheted off three walls.

But more than that, Maud's behaviour during that arduous journey opened my eyes to the danger of giving one's affection to a woman before she has proved herself worthy of it. She repeatedly tried to pretend that it was all my fault. My fault! As if *I* had made her wear the fatal ear-rings! And she did nothing but grizzle and complain – and, of course, sniff. She complained when, with a new authority I had somehow acquired, I persuaded old Mr Toddy to cart us part of the way in his wheelbarrow. She moaned at me when cars refused to give us a hitch-hike into Margate – it wasn't my fault, it was the fault of the stuff we had to lie on in the bottom of the wheelbarrow.

And she even carried on when I finally got Mr Parkinson to drive us all the way to the hospital, even though we could lie down comfortably in the back of his vehicle, bracing ourselves against the coffin.

I used to see Maud from time to time after that day and we would chat civilly enough but my passion was spent; I had grown up.

Sometimes, as I was strolling through the town with a younger, more impressionable friend, he would spot Maud leaning up against the wall and ask eagerly, 'Hey, who's that leaning up against the wall?'

'That?' I would say, a light, sophisticated smile playing about the corners of my mouth:

'Maud, bored, and dangerous to gnaw.'

DNDNDNDNDNDNDNDNDNDN

A nod is as good as a wink to a blind horse

R. H. Barham
'The Ingoldsby Legends'

N 1942, I was a Wop. Before I get either a reproachful letter from the Race Relations people or a Welcome Home card from the Mafia, let me explain that term. In 1942, a 'Wop' was the RAF abbreviation for 'Wireless Operator', and that was what Daddy did in World War Two. (Oh, come on, child, you've heard of World War Two, it starred Leslie Banks.) I was 1615358, Wireless Operator U/T: U/T being another ingenious RAF abbreviation. It stood for 'Under Training'.

About that training. The RAF had calculated that the maximum period necessary to transform even the most irresolute of civilians into a red-hot Wireless Operator was three months. At the time we are considering, I had been Under Training for a year and a half.

That, again, needs some explanation. You see, before the RAF would allow you to Operate a Wireless for them, you had to pass two completely different examinations. They were both designed to test your skill at reading Morse Code signals.

The first one tested whether you could read them aurally. That, if I've spelt the word right, does not mean through your mouth – but through your ears. What happened was, you put on a wireless headset and translated any Morse bleeps you heard into letters of the alphabet.

Of the two tests, that was the one I had no trouble with. In fact, I can still do it. To this day, I find myself 'hearing' Morse in all sorts of things. Remember the 'Dragnet' theme – 'Dum . . . di-*dum*-dum!'? To my ears, that still comes out as 'Dah . . . di-*dah*-dit', which is Morse Code for 'T.R.' Useful facility, isn't it?

No, it was the second test which, as far as Wireless Operating was concerned, turned me into what we now call a late developer. In this test you had to prove that you could read Morse 'visually'.

Let me describe what that entailed. They stood you on top of a hill, from which you gazed across a valley at another hill. On top of that hill stood the Senior NCO we called 'Fanny', for reasons which memory has blurred.

He operated what was known as an Aldis lamp, a sort of lantern with movable shutters in front. He blinked this on and off at you. The alternations of long blinks of light and short blinks of light formed the Morse Code letters which the RAF expected you, at that distance, to distinguish, translate and write down.

I couldn't even see them. To me, the whole operation was just a vaguely luminous, slightly shimmering, blur.

There was good reason for this. A reason immediately apparent to any of you who've ever seen me in that temple of peculiar pleasure, the flesh. The most dominant feature is the glasses with the thick black frames. I wear them nowadays not, as some have supposed, to de-emphasise the deep eye-sockets but to stop me bumping into things. Like office blocks.

In *those* days, however ... in 1942! Well, I was only going on for twenty, wasn't I? There were girls! I mean, did anyone ever see Robert Taylor wearing *glasses*? Not even when he was playing a scientist.

So that was why, long before the Beatles were even born, I was known to Fanny as 'the fool on the hill'. Never mind not being able to distinguish the blinks of his Aldis lamp – I could barely make out the intervening valley.

I could well have remained Under Training until the Yalta Conference. The reason why I didn't can be summed up in the words of another Beatles' song: 'I get by with a little help from my friends'. Specifically, the other trainees on that 1942 course.

Mind you, it wasn't easy for them to help me. Regulations demanded that the rest of the class stood at least ten yards behind the trainee taking the test – so that no Hawkeye among them could *whisper* the letters to him as they were being blinked out.

So what they did was this. They put themselves in possession of a very long stick of bamboo. 'Liberated' it, as we then used to say. Then, as each letter was flashed at me, they prodded that stick into the small of my back. Soft-prod for a short blink of the lamp, hard-prod for a long blink.

If we return to that Dragnet example, in bamboo-stick terms it becomes 'HARD ... Soft-*HARD*-soft'. Are you with me? So was good fortune. I passed out top of the entry.

Admittedly, I still have to see the osteopath once a week. And, what's more, paying for the visit out of my own pocket. Although I could well present the damaged spinal column to authority as an authentic war wound, to do so might spoil someone else's chances. Because, so I've been told, the ploy is still operating in the RAF.

Even today, RAF trainees who have trouble making out what visual signals are being shone into their short-sighted eyes, are being rescued by that same system of dig-in-the-back simultaneous translation. The lads have even adapted a proverb to cover the situation:

A prod is as good as a blink to a shined Morse.

FMFMFMFMFMFMFMFMFMFMFM

So he passed over, and all the trumpets sounded for
him on the other side

John Bunyan
'Pilgrim's Progress'

A FEW weeks ago the publisher, Mark Bonham Carter, was
walking in Hyde Park when he heard somebody calling his
name, 'Mark! Mark!' He turned and there was nobody there.
He walked on a little and again he heard a small rather quer-
ulous voice call, 'Mark! Mark! Mark!' Then he looked
downwards and there at his ankles was a small dog with a hare lip.

I mention the incident as a demonstration of the peculiar quality
which names have for being other things.

I mean, did you know that the Victoria and Albert Museum was
named after two people? Well, it was. It was named after the men
who founded it, Frank Mu and Alastair Seum.

And take Strip-Tease. Were you aware that Strip-Tease was named
after the man who imported it into this country at the fag-end of the
last century, Phineas Stripp? Well, it was. It had no name in France but
when Phineas imported the idea he hired a theatre in London in between the matinee and the evening performance and served tea while
the ladies divested. These became known as Stripp Teas, and the name
stuck.

The story of how Phineas, a poor boy with dreams, beat the great
impresarios at their own game is gripping. Not very funny, but gripping. Well, not very gripping really; say, semi-gripping.

He had heard tell from travellers that a new form of entertainment
was sweeping the halls of Calais and Dieppe. A number of girls were
engaged – chiefly from the ranks of unemployed clog-chisellers – and
each was provided with a pair of stout, iron button-hooks. Then, to
the inflammatory music of Offenbach, the girls stood on stage and
proceeded to unbutton their dresses. As at that time the dresses were
done up with over three hundred buttons the process took about an
hour and a half. The girls then posed for an intoxicating moment in an

undershift of bullet-proof mauve bombazine reaching from shin to neck and the customers reeled out into the night air with steam coming out of their ears.

Phineas set to work. He persuaded a theatre manager to lend him a theatre in exchange for two pounds in cash, a second-hand overcoat with a fur collar and first crack at the lady clog-chisellers. Next Phineas had suitable music written for him, on tick, by the composer Hubert Seldom-Byte. His name is not remembered much now but in those days Seldom-Byte was the English equivalent of Offenbach.

It was at that point that young Phineas came up against a snag. His next move was to travel across the channel to Calais and audition a batch of unbuttoners. Although of tender years Phineas had been through the School of Hard Knocks and he had no illusions about the girls: he was fully aware that any unemployed clog-chisellers prepared to parade themselves stark-naked from the shin down and the neck up were No Better Than They Ought To Be, and would need to be carefully selected if he was to get them past Customs.

But he had no money for the fare to Calais.

A lesser man might have given up at this point. For a moment Phineas did contemplate returning to his old job of sprinkling tinsel on coloured picture-postcards of Lord Palmerston but British grit won through. He decided to swim. Or rather, as he could not swim, to float.

It was bitterly cold on Broadstairs beach that morning when, watched by a small group of weeping creditors, Phineas prepared to take to the waves. He had provided himself with twenty yards of string upon which he had threaded eight hundred medicine-bottle corks. With a creditor holding one end of the string, Phineas tied the other end just below his knee then spun round like a tee-to-tum until he had wound himself up in the corks and string. He sang out a cheery farewell, hopped to the water's edge and fell in.

He floated rather well. In a moment the tide had caught him and along the coast he went, his brave figure getting smaller and smaller to the tense watchers on the beach.

Half an hour later his brave figure began to get larger and larger. Just when he was approaching Dover the tide had changed and swept him back to Broadstairs.

The following morning he tried again: the same thing happened. Forty-eight attempts he made that long, hot summer and never once got beyond Dover before being returned by the changing tide.

Then came the breakthrough. One day he was standing next to the plate-glass window of a toy-shop – just reflecting – when he glanced within. There, in the window, a tiny boat was being demonstrated. It skeetered busily around a plateful of water propelled by a tiny chip of camphor at its rear end.

'Europa!' cried Phineas (who had little Greek). 'That's my answer!'

In a trice he had purchased from a ladies' outfitters a voluminous undergarment pioneered by Mrs Amelia Bloomer for the use of lady bicyclists. He put double-strength elastic in where the garment gripped below the knees, climbed in, and poured half a hundredweight of fresh camphor balls in at the rear. It was but the work of a moment to wind himself up in the string and corks and totter into the briny.

What a difference this time. There was a fizzing and a bubbling behind him and he found himself zig-zagging erratically round Broadstairs harbour. Fortunately all the Stripp family were noted for their enormous, spatula-like feet and Phineas found that by moving his feet this way and that they made a pair of fine rudders, giving him perfect steering control. He straightened up and, to a muffled cheer from the beach, settled down to a steady eight knots on a course of roughly SE by S.

So . . . well, the rest is show-biz history (see *Decline and Fall of the Holborn Empire*, Eddy Gibbon, vol. 4, chap. 8).

So he passed Dover, and all the strumpets undid for him on the other side.

Charity shall cover the multitude of sins

The New Testament
First Epistle General of Peter

I HAPPENED to drop into my club last week – it's the Odeon Saturday Morning Club, I try to get in there about once a month – and, while the adverts were on, I got chatting to the fellow sitting next to me. He made a disconcerting observation about the way I tell these stories on the 'My Word!' radio programmes. 'Do you realise,' he said, 'you have a very . . . slow . . . delivery.'

Now that's a strangely uncomfortable thing to have pointed out about yourself, that you've got a very slow delivery. It makes you feel like a delinquent laundryman. Or an inexperienced gynaecologist. Although this chap went on to explain that all he meant was that my mode of utterance seems inordinately deliberate and emphatic, that only made me feel worse. You see, I know the reason *why* I talk like that when on the wireless. And there is no way of making that reason sound like an achievement.

It's because, on these broadcasting occasions, I am invariably drunk. Oh, not 'I'll fight any man in the room' drunk, not even 'I've brought nothing but unhappiness to everybody who's ever had anything to do with me' drunk – just 'unless I say this word slowly it won't come out right' drunk.

It's all a result of something that happened to me about the time I reached forty. Some kind of chemical change took place in my – it's all right, you can do these four-letter words now – body. I don't know exactly what happened but, almost overnight, the absolute minimum of alcohol suddenly become sufficient to start me yodelling. Isn't it terrible to be struck down like that in the prime of life? Without any prior warning, I became a secret non-drinker.

What made that almost a professional disaster, however, was that the alteration in my metabolism coincided almost exactly with the tenth year of the 'My Word!' series. Let me explain the significance of that anniversary: when a radio programme has been on the air for ten years, it thereafter becomes eligible for what the BBC calls 'hospitality';

henceforth, the Corporation provides drinks for the cast before the programme. Mind you, when I say 'drinks', perhaps I should be more precise. Five slim-line tonic-waters, and a bottle of gin which you are allowed to drink down as far as the pencil-mark. So there I was, invited at last to drink at the BBC's expense – but, at the same time, rendered physically incapable of accepting the invitation.

Why couldn't I simply stick to tonic-water, you may ask. To answer that, one has to understand the workings of a public corporation. If they were to discover that their bottle of gin was not being drunk down to the pencilled-level indicated, Accounts Department would then embark on what's called 'revising the estimate'. The following week, we'd find the pencil-mark an inch higher up the bottle. And, in Show Business, status is all. The first question any member of one BBC programme asks a representative of another programme is, 'How far down the bottle is your pencil-mark?'

'All right,' you might acknowledge, 'then why don't you just give your gins to one of the other people in the show?' Answer: it would only create worse problems. I mean, which one could I give them to? Certainly not Dilys Powell or Anne Scott-James. Look, you know from films what lady newspaper-columnists are like. Think of Glenda Farrell, Eve Arden, Rosalind Russell – tough, cynical, suspicious. Way their minds work, any man who starts offering them buckshee gins, he's only after one thing.

Jack Longland, then? No, it just wouldn't be right. You can't offer additional gins to a man who has to drive his wife all the way back to Derbyshire after every programme. It's already difficult enough for him to negotiate those motorways with someone sitting on his cross-bar.

Frank Muir? Oh, come on. . . ! I know Frank's alcoholic reactions as well as I know my own. When he goes on to perform, he is already at the very frontier of his capacity. One more gin and he'd be rolling up his trouser-legs and putting on Dilys's hat.

No, for the welfare of the team, for the sake of the programme, I cannot do other than swallow those gins myself. Even though it results in my performing every show with my upper lip gone numb and my tongue feeling like it's got too large to fit my mouth.

That's the reason for my slow delivery. The only way I can disguise the fact that I have consumed more alcohol than my body can now deal with is to articulate very slowly and . . . very . . . CLEARLY. In the hope that, as the Good Book almost has it:

'Clarity shall cover the multitude of gins.'

And so to bed

Samuel Pepys
'Diary'

'OH, botheration!' exclaimed Drusilla Kennington-Oval, her gamine face puckering at the corners in a tiny moue of vexation. She had come to the end of her novel, *Heartsease*, by Monica Liphook (Olympia Press), and it was time for her to get out of bed and face another mad, jolly, gorgeous day.

She widened her slim, artistic fingers, and a thumb, and the book slipped to the cottage floor with an unaccustomed plonk. In a trice she was out of bed, long limbs flashing, and down on her knees mopping up the plonk – a bottle of agreeable but cheap Yugoslav Chablis which she was trying out.

It was nearly half-past ten and already she could hear her farmer neighbours beginning to stir; the slam of a shooting-brake door as one set off for a round of golf; the cheerful clatter of helicopter blades as another was whisked away to some dreary old business meeting in Brussels.

Not wanting to miss a minute of glorious sunshine Dru flung on an old pair of patched jeans, thrust her feet into an old pair of patched moccasins and ran down to her front gate.

'Hello, Mr Helicopter Pilot!' she cried gaily, waving both her arms high in the air. 'Bon voyage!'

The helicopter hit a tree.

Biting her lip at her silly forgetfulness she ran back into the cottage and flung on an old patched bra and an old patched sweater.

Dru never was much of a one for breakfast. Just a spoonful or two of game pâté flung onto an old Bath Oliver biscuit and she was running like a deer over the familiar hillocks and meadows of Platt's Bottom, breathing in the pure country air – she loved breathing – stopping only for a quick draw on a fag or a chat with a cow.

And then ... suddenly, there was Derwent Hilliton. A moment before, the lane had been empty. But, now. There was Derwent Hilliton in his new Maserati, forty feet long and nine inches high. Derwent ...

'Hi, you!' said Derwent, in his usual laconic fashion. He was wiping a speck of dust from the steering-wheel with a ten pound note. Once again Dru was conscious of the sheer animal magnetism which exuded from his every pore. As ever, she caught her breath at his fabulous profile, which he was holding so that she could admire it. There was something almost feminine in his grace of movement as he folded the banknote and put it back into his handbag.

'This is good-bye, Dru.' He said, all of a sudden.

'But ...' gasped Dru, 'Why ...? What ...? Who ...? When ...? If ...? Could ...? Is ...? How ...? Can ...?'

'Father has just given me a million pounds to make good on my own. I'm off to Tibet tomorrow to build a luxury hotel; the Shangri-La-Hilliton.'

'I see. At least, I think I see.'

'But it doesn't have to be good-bye. Will you come, Dru? As Mrs Hilliton. Think it over. I'll ring you tonight.'

With a muffled roar from the gold-plated twin-exhausts, he was gone.

Dru's heart was in a turmoil; lickety-spit, lickety-spit, it went. Did she really love him? Did he really love her? What to do?

As ever when she was troubled she found that her feet had taken her to Blair Tremayne's cottage, at the back of the 'Dog and Duck'.

And as ever her heart skipped a beat at the simple, bachelor scene inside. An old tennis racquet lying just where he had used it for draining the chips. An old army boot full of cold porridge ready for an early breakfast. The old-fashioned wooden mangle he used for getting the last scrap of toothpaste out of the tube.

For Blair had no father to give him a million pounds. He was just a humble, dedicated writer, hard at work translating a French/English dictionary into English/French. But so kind. And reliable. And ...

A muffled grunt made her turn, and there was Blair towering over her. He folded her in his arms twice – he had rather long arms – and hugged her tightly to him.

His tweed jacket smelled deliciously of old spaniel dog.

'Dru,' he gasped, throatily. 'Dru. Oh, Dru ...'

Releasing one hand, he removed an old spaniel dog from beneath his jacket.

'Oh, Dru. Dru.'

Blair was a man of few words and had to work those he knew rather hard.

'Dru. Me. And you, Dru. Marry? Eh, Dru? May I be Mr Drusilla Kennington-Oval?'

With a half-cry, Dru freed herself from his dear arms. She had to have time to think. So she walked, and walked. All that day she walked. Through fields, along roads; she knew not where. At one time she thought she recognised the Manchester Ship Canal. Another time she was hailed by a friend in the foyer of the Royal Albion Hotel, Bognor Regis. But she walked on.

When she arrived back at her little cottage there were two bunches of flowers waiting for her. Five hundred orchids tied with satin ribbon bore a card, 'Say yes. Derwent.' Three daisies tied together with fuse-wire bore a piece of tissue paper, 'Be mine. Blair.'

Which to choose? When she opened the curtains on the morning of the honeymoon was she to see the massive glaciers of far-off Tibet? Or an army boot full of cold porridge and a view of the Gents at the back of the 'Dog and Duck?'

Gentle reader, can you doubt her choice?

Dru made her decision. She was wedded and bedded. And on the first morning she flung back the curtains of her bedroom window ...

And saw Tibet.

DNDNDNDNDNDNDNDNDN

It is better to be envied than pitied

Ancient Greek Proverb

ONE of the more depressing of middle-life experiences, not that most of them aren't, is trying on your old RAF uniform and finding that the only part of it that still fits you is the tie. That's why my attention perked up at one of the adverts in my local cinema.

'Men!' it said, the exclamation-mark blinking on and off, 'Are you finding yourself with more waist, less speed? Then join our Health Club.' The accompanying visuals displayed a variety of narrow-hipped prematurely-greys vaulting easily over wooden horses, exchanging pleasantries in Our Organic Juice Bar and roaring off in open cars with droopy girls running fingertips up their forearm.

I joined the following day. The name of the Club escapes me now, but it was something out of mythology – 'Priam', or 'Priapus', the kind of allusion that's been popularised by all those classical scholars now on a retainer to advertising agencies for the naming of male deodorants. What I do recall is that the place was a former slaughter-house and that the young man who greeted me wore one of those thick rollneck sweaters I still associate with U-Boat captains. He also had the kind of handshake that ought never to be used except as a tourniquet. It took me a good four minutes to get my knuckles back in line.

His first move was to sell me, for a price I would normally expect to pay for a winter overcoat, a pair of gym shorts and a cotton singlet. After I'd changed into them, I presented myself before him for inspection. All right, admittedly not an impressive sight but, for heaven's sake, hardly deserving the performance he put on.

'Oh dear, oh lor,' he kept repeating. He was walking round me slowly and respectfully, as one does at Hadrian's Villa or Pompeii, any of the places where the guidebooks use the phrase 'ruined grandeur'. 'Oh, you have let yourself go, haven't you,' he said finally.

23

'I have,' I said. 'And I enjoyed it. Both times.'

'Not to worry, old-timer. We'll soon have you leaping about again. Be the fittest sixty-year-old down your street.'

'I'm forty-six,' I said. But by this time he had me in among the rest of the class.

Well, I don't like to appear condescending, but honestly, repulsive really is the only word. Not one of them could have been a day under forty-eight or fifty. Watching all of them wheezing about in those baggy shorts and the singlets with 'I Am The Greatest' across the chest, I couldn't help but give the U-Boat captain a rueful wink, which he affected not to notice.

No one can say that, over the next hour, I didn't co-operate fully in all that bend, stretch, lift, pull, lie flat, run on the spot, up-up-up-up, everybody jump on everybody else's back. Nor did I fail to pull my weight during all the succeeding Wednesdays and Fridays that I joined the old crocks there at what I soon came privately to refer to as 'Hernia's Hideaway'.

I even did, twice a day in the privacy of my office, the special P.T. homework which the Club asked of me. As instructed, I bent forward, grasped the ends of my two feet firmly and, without letting go, did pull-pull-pull for a full quarter of an hour. As far as I could tell, the only noticeable result was that, two months later, I'd gone from a size ten shoe to a size twelve.

It was not till he got me on to weight-lifting that breaking-point was reached. Holding between his thumb and forefinger a thick iron bar with two enormous discs at either end, he said, 'Righto then, your turn.'

I looked behind me. 'It's you I'm talking to,' he said. 'The Phyllosan Kid. Let's see a standing snatch. Take your time.'

I won't have anyone accuse me of not trying. I spat on my hands, bent down, took a firm grip, jammed my back-teeth together, tightened my stomach muscles, bore down on my heels, and did a sharp, powerful snatch. For eight minutes. At which point he said, 'Not bad for first time. Friday we'll see if you can lift it as far as your ankles. Go and have a shower now.'

I put a question to him. 'Have you got the kind of shower that has its nozzle in the ground, so that the water squirts vertically upwards?'

'What do you want one of them for?'

'Because I can't straighten up.'

No more could I. Well into the autumn I was still moving around in a kind of Groucho Marx lope. If Physical Training is the price you have to pay for Physical Fitness, I'll settle for pooped. Those Ancient Greeks knew what they were talking about:

It is better to be unfit than P.T.'d.

FMFMFMFMFMFMFMFMFM

The lamps are going out all over Europe

Edward, Viscount Grey of Fallodon
3 Aug. 1914

THE Most Unforgettable Character I ever met was – well, he's dead now and I don't remember much about him. On the other hand, the Most Forgettable Character I ever met is most memorable. He was elected Most Forgettable Character by our form at school. The craze for electing the Most Something-or-other had hit our form heavily that year – I was, I recall elected the Most Smelly, an injustice which has rankled ever since. But the application of the word 'forgettable' to Oliver Sinclair Yarrop was only too appropriate. I can see him now, a veal-faced lad with no colour about him anywhere; his hair was the same colour as his skin, which was colourless; he had almost transparent ears. He took no interest at all in the normal pursuits of healthy schoolboys, like boasting loudly, spitting, eating, punching girls: his sole passion in life was the love, and care, of animals.

It is a melancholy fact, which as schoolboys we but dimly perceived, that Dame Fate is a cruel Jade; and one of her little caprices is to allow a growing lad to work up a lifetime ambition whilst at the same time making sure that he is totally unequipped to achieve it. Thus my best friend, Nigel Leatherbarrow, wanted to be the Pope: he was Jewish. And my second-best-friend, Tarquin Wilson, wanted to be a girl. And I wanted to be rich. But the worst example was poor little, Forgettable Oliver; he desperately wanted to be a vet, and as much as he loved animals, they loathed him.

I, interested in people but indifferent to furred and feathered beasts, was beloved by the animal kingdom. Even now I cannot walk very far before dogs appear from nowhere and sniff my socks. When I return home I find a nest of field mice in my turn-ups. I have only to pause a moment to lean up against a tree and ladybirds settle on me in such numbers that I look as if I have galloping chicken pox.

But all animal life viewed Oliver with implacable hatred. Full of love for them, he would hold out his left hand for every dog to sniff. When he left school the fingers of his left hand were an inch shorter than those of his right hand. Every pullover he possessed was lacerated by kittens' claws. One of his jackets had lost a shoulder where a cow had taken a bite at him. His right shin bore the scar where a chicken had driven her beak in. Animals had bitten him so much that when I saw him, for the last time, stripped for gym, he looked deckle-edged.

I did not see Oliver again until after the war. I was at an RAF hospital in the country being treated for shock – brought on by the realisation that I was about to be demobilised and would have to work for a living – and on a country walk I suddenly came upon Oliver. He had his back to a brick wall and was being attacked by a duckling. Unclamping the bird's beak from Oliver's ankle I fell to talking. He had changed considerably since we had last met. He no longer wore his school cap and long trousers covered his bony, unmemorable knees. He seemed middle-aged before his time. He had on one of those gingery, very thick tweed suits with bits in them which look as though they had been woven from marmalade. His hair was very thin; almost emaciated. And he only had one arm.

It seems that he gave up all hopes of becoming a vet when he realised that the exams meant maths. But an aunt died, leaving him a little money – she was a member of an obscure religious sect; he assured me that she had returned to earth and still lived with him in the form of a stuffed airedale – and he had decided to spend the rest of his life in tending animals in an amateur way. For that purpose he went for little walks, always carrying with him a thermometer and a used lolly-stick so that when he encountered an animal he could make it say 'Aaah!' and take its temperature. It was work he loved.

But, he confessed with a sudden flush, he had not as yet managed to examine an animal. No sooner had he pressed his used lolly-stick on the little, or large, or forked tongue than the creature sank its teeth into the nearest available piece of Oliver and was away. Not one 'Aaah!' had he achieved.

And worse than that, a blow from a robin's wing had lost him his arm. Oliver was up a ladder at the time, trying to take the temperature of this robin who was on a branch of an apple-tree. Apparently Oliver thought the robin looked rather flushed so approached it with his lolly-stick and said 'say "Aaah!" ' whereupon the robin flapped a wing which dislodged an apple which fell upon Oliver's fingers and he let go of the ladder.

Less obvious but just as regrettable was the loss of his left big toe when the tortoise he was trying to examine fell from his hands, and the loss of two medium toes on his right foot due to circumstances which I did not quite grasp but which entailed a rabbit and Oliver wearing green socks.

That was the last time I saw what was left of Oliver alive. I read an account of his passing over in a local paper I was folding up the other day (I had a hole in my shoe and it was coming on to rain). The newspaper report said that Oliver Sinclair Yarrop had bent down with a lolly-stick to a young lamb and was trying to persuade it to say 'Aaah!'. What Oliver had not noticed was that there was a large goat just behind him. But the goat had noticed Oliver. And the temptation was too great. It had charged.

As the coroner said, it was not the butt which hurt Oliver so much as the landing, which took an appreciable time to occur during which time Oliver was accelerating at the rate of thirty-two feet per sec. per sec. But what did the deceased think he was doing, fooling about with a lamb on the edge of Beachy Head?

So the Forgettable Oliver died, and is almost forgotten. But if there is a hereafter, and I think there is, he will be happy at last. There will be green fields there. And hundreds and hundreds of little woolly lambs.

And more than that:

The lambs are going 'Aaah!' to Oliver Yarrop.

DNDNDNDNDNDNDNDNDNDN

Oh the little more, and how much it is

Robert Browning
'By the Fireside'

SOME time ago Frank Muir and I wrote a television series which turned out so dire that one newspaper considered reviewing it in the obituary column. The comment which caused Frank most distress, however, appeared in a Sunday rag. 'It is now obvious that Muir and Norden have exhibited themselves so frequently as performers, they no longer possess any ability to write. They are now to be regarded merely as talkers.'

I cannot recall ever seeing my colleague more choked. 'Do you realise,' he said, 'do you realise the implications if what that paper says is true? Bang go my chances for Posterity. And you know how I feel about Posterity.'

I do. He's very keen on it. 'When I go,' he said, 'I want to be remembered.'

'Well, I'll remember you,' I said. 'I bet I will. Burly chap with a bow-tie. Swiped my felt-nib pen.'

'Nobody'd call you Posterity, would they? I'm talking about real *afterwards* Posterity. "Merely talkers!" What a shameful rotten thing for a paper to write. Name me one "talker" who's been remembered by Posterity. Eh? Name me one! Yes, all right, Dr Johnson. But he had Boswell, didn't he. All I've got is you.'

Frank is inclined to do that. Ask you a question, answer it himself, then tell you you were wrong. This time, however, something different happened. He suddenly sat up and stared at me. Then – 'Sir,' he said. 'Sir, it may be that you will suffice.'

He had never called me 'Sir' before. Within the tundra of my heart, something thawed and started trickling. 'Dear old Frank,' I said. 'What are you chuntering on about?'

'Boswell and Johnson,' he said. 'Boswell just followed Johnson around everywhere and jotted down every observation Johnson uttered into

29

a notebook. Then he transferred all the notebook stuff into five volumes and came up with *Boswell's Life Of Dr Johnson*. One of the all-time Posterity chart-toppers! Well, why can't you do the same thing?'

'Because,' I said, 'I think he's dead. We could check with the British Medical Council, but they must have so many Dr Johnsons on their –'

'Sir,' Frank said. 'Follow me more closely. *Norden's Life of Mr Muir!* Using exactly the same technique. By cracky, the more I think about it, the more I like it. Can you give me a good reason why we can't start right away?'

'I think so,' I said. 'I haven't got a notebook.'

'Sir,' Frank said, and one could tell he was already living the part. 'Sir, you will need more than one notebook. Five volumes at, say, three hundred pages per each, let's see.' He stabbed expertly at his pocket-calculator. Then he took it out of his pocket and stabbed again. When we'd checked the answer with my Ready Reckoner, we set off for that Office Stationery shop in Maddox Street. The manager, I thought, seemed a little anxious when we explained ourselves.

'Sir,' Frank said, not only living it now but loving it. 'Sir, I am Mr Muir and this is my biographer. Do you stock those 3p notebooks with a spiral wire going up and down the spine?' We had agreed that those would be the best form of notebook for me to carry, as they wouldn't spoil the shape of my good suit when accompanying Frank to coffee-houses or journeys to the Highlands.

'I think I can find you one,' the manager said.

'Sir,' Frank said, 'eight hundred and seventy.'

One thing about that manager, he did help stack the eight hundred and seventy notebooks inside a wooden crate, in order to make them easier for me to carry. I say 'me' because, as Frank pointed out, if he were to give a hand in the humping about of a dirty great wooden crate, how would he have the puff to utter any observations for me to copy down.

As we tauntered back along Regent Street – 'taunter' is a labour-saving word I'm using to describe the appearance of one person saun-tering, the other tottering – so clement and agreeable was the autumnal sunshine that Frank was moved to utter Observation One.

'Sir,' he observed, 'could the fact that new cars are invariably intro-duced in the autumn be the reason why they are sometimes known as autumnobiles?'

Unfortunately, the blood was now pounding so hard in my ears, I didn't hear what he said. 'Do what?' I asked.

'I just did an observation,' Frank said.

'Sorry. Hang about.' I lowered the wooden crate to the pavement and took out the top notebook. 'Sir,' Frank said, 'could the fact that new cars are invariably introduced in the why aren't you writing any of this down?'

'You've still got my felt-nib pen.'

He threw it at me. 'Get it down while it's fresh.'

I wrote feverishly then stopped. 'I didn't really hear what you said.' A few people had now gathered round us. 'Please,' I said to Frank, 'just one more time.'

As he reiterated it, very slowly this time and quite loudly, I wrote it carefully into the notebook. While I was doing so, a small elderly lady plucked at my sleeve. 'Excuse me, officer,' she said. 'What are you charging him with?'

Now it must have happened during the time that I was explaining to that lady that I was not a plain-clothes policeman, I was a biographer just starting on the first page of the first notebook of a five-volume biography, it must have been while I was busy doing that that some alert mafioso swiped the wooden crate.

That is the reason why the publication of the not-much-heralded *Norden's Life Of Mr Muir* has been unavoidably delayed. The fact is, all I have of it to date is one measly observation and a bill for eight hundred and seventy spiral wire notebooks at 3p each which comes to a sum of no less than would you believe £26.10. As Browning damn near got round to commenting:

'Oh, the little Muir, and how much it is!'

FMFMFMFMFMFMFMFMFMFM

I was desolate and sick of an old passion

Ernest Dowson
'Non Sum Qualis Eram'

HAVE rather gone off Denis Norden. One does go off people from time to time. Other people I have been off (off whom I have been?) include Crippen, Hitler, Mrs Mary Whitehouse, Pontius Pilate, Patrick Campbell, Professor A. L. Rowse and Charlie Chaplin, so Denis is in good company. It's just that he was a bit infuriating this afternoon.

We had arranged to meet at his office at 3 p.m. on a matter of business – he was trying to sell me a camera which he had dropped – and when I arrived at seven minutes past the hour he said to me, with a trace of irritability in his normally suave voice, 'You're late.'

Well, I mean to say. He was the cause of it. Just as I was leaving home I received this garbled message from his secretary, Hedda Garbler, saying that Denis had been having lunch at a Chinese restaurant and had left something there which belonged to his aunt and would I pick it up on my way in and thank you.

Ever the one to oblige an old friend I dropped in to the restaurant and collected the thing, of which the management was visibly glad to be relieved, which appeared to be a rolled-up, dark grey, very tatty sheepskin rug – and rather smelly with it.

I proceeded blithely along Kensington High Street in an easterly direction, playing with the thing the way one does when carrying a thing – tossing it in the air and catching it, punting it along the pavement for a bit, shoving it under the arm and carrying it like a rugger ball – when I realised that it was giving off warmth. This was a little alarming so I stopped and began to unwrap the bundle. Or rather, I tried to unwrap the bundle. It was not a bundle. Or a rolled-up rug. It was a very, very old, mangy Persian cat.

Now I am not a cat man. I am unable to exchange minds with a cat. Sigmund Freud spent thirty years researching into the feminine soul

32

before confessing that he could find no answer to the question: what does a woman *want*? I feel the same sense of inadequacy with a cat.

I looked at the cat and the cat returned the favour with a steady look of cold, implacable malevolence.

I decided upon a show of strength.

'All right, Moggy,' I said firmly, 'let's go.'

She gave a sort of sweep with one arm and my hair had four partings in it.

Cats have these scimitars built into their paws for just this sort of aggro and my old lady had hers locked in the 'attack' position. A sharp pain in my side told me that she was putting in some serious work on my jacket – obviously trying to get at my liver.

In a flash I grabbed her by the neck and stuffed her into my jacket pocket. I left her head sticking out so that she could breathe but by clamping my hand against the pocket I had her tightly pinioned.

'Get out of that!' I chortled.

I felt her go rigid. I realised later that she went rigid when she was thinking things out; planning her next move.

It came just as I was about level with the Albert Hall. My right thigh began to grow hot. Then it grew cold. And my right ankle felt distinctly damp.

She had gained the initiative once again.

Hoisting her out of my pocket by the neck and holding her at arm's length I nipped into that little ironmonger's shop near Albert Hall Mansions, bought a ball of shiny string, tied one end round her neck and paid out the string until I had her on a ten-yard-long lead. My thinking was that by the time she had run that ten yards, scimitars bared, I would have had a chance to take evasive action.

She was furious. She immediately went rigid, pondering, and I was able to make quite a bit of distance, dragging her along on the end of the string.

She got my measure just as we came up to Hyde Park Corner. There was a quick flurry of fur and she emerged out of her trance like a streak of lightning, tearing round and round me in a clockwise direction. I couldn't think what she was up to at first but I soon found out. In a moment she had me trussed up in string like a mummy. I teetered for a second, trying to keep my balance, but, very gently, she gave a little pull on the string and I crashed to the ground.

I extricated myself from the string and then it was I who went rigid. After some thought it seemed to me that I should not attempt the impossible, i.e. to outwit the cat or overcome it by strength, but concentrate on solving the immediate problem: how to prevent myself from being wound up in the string and brought crashing to the pavement every few yards. As the cat acted – I would have to react.

And so that is how we proceeded along the length of Piccadilly and into Denis's office, in a kind of screw movement; the cat sprinting round me in a clockwise direction while I sprinted round the cat in an anti-clockwise direction.

I arrived at seven minutes past the hour and he said 'You're late'. Can you wonder that I have gone off him?

Indeed I was late. But I was a little more than late.

I was dizzy, late and sick of an old Persian.

DNDNDNDNDNDNDNDNDNDN

Hope springs eternal in the human breast

Alexander Pope
'Essay on Criticism'

F you saw, some months ago, a rather tangled version of this quotation headlining *The Times* music critic's column, I'm afraid that was my fault. It was the outcome of an incident where I saved a young Dutch girl from being mowed down by a runaway hors d'œuvre trolley.

What happened was, I was having lunch with an American producer who'd had the idea of making a film called *Marty*, to be based on the life of Luther. And while he was going on about it, I saw an hors d'œuvre trolley start to move forward.

Now as you know, in elegant London hotels the hors d'œuvre trolleys are always about the size of small trams. As, at this place, the dining-room floor also had a slight incline, once the trolley got rolling, it gathered speed at an enormous lick and, in no time, was hurtling down the room, rocking and swaying and spilling out Russian salad and sardines.

Then I noticed something else. Directly in its path was this girl. To make matters worse, she happened to be bending forward – not consciously, I don't think, she just had rather heavy ear-rings on. Anyway, without even thinking, I dived forward and swept her aside. The great trolley hurtled past and splattered itself harmlessly against an elderly waiter. (A team of surgeons, I've been told, were still picking black olives out of him six hours later.)

The girl's husband, a prosperous Dutchman, was quite embarrassingly grateful. Apparently, they'd only been married three days and were having a week's honeymoon in London. So if that trolley had claimed her, it would have been a really rotten waste of a double room.

'Mijnheer,' he said to me, with more emotion than I had thought the Dutch capable of, 'for what you have done, I will send to you the largest token of my gratitude that my craftsmen can manufacture.'

All right, what would you have reckoned he had in mind? So did I. Cupidity glands started extruding like icing-bags. Seven complete days passed before it was borne upon me that diamond-cutting is not the only craft for which the Dutch are renowned.

The reminder came from the man from British Rail Services. When I opened the door of my flat to him, he said, 'It won't go in the lift and I'm not humping it up them stairs.'

I accompanied him down to the entrance hall and there it was. A cheese. A Dutch cheese, the size of – look, do you remember that cartwheel Bernard Miles used to lean on? Well, imagine something the same diameter, but about two feet thick and bright red.

I stood gazing at it for quite some time. As it happens, I am allergic to cheese. It dates back to an incident in my boyhood when I pulled on a pair of swimming trunks, inside which someone had left a loaded mouse-trap.

So I said to the van man, 'Can't you possibly take it away again? Share it out among the lads?'

He turned out to be one of those people who talk in A's and B's. 'A,' he said, 'I'm not ruining myself trying to lift that thing up again, B, how would anyone cut it?'

It was then I had a brainwave. In Flat 14, there was this young musician, a student at the Royal Academy of Music. And what was he studying? The harp.

Do I need to spell out the rest of it? After all, in existential terms, what is a harp but an oversized cheese-slicer with cultural pretensions?

In the event, it worked a treat. The van man had no trouble carrying the Dutch treasure away in lightweight slices and, no doubt, his depot is still acclaimed for the lavishness of its wine-and-cheese parties.

And that should have been the end of the story. But unfortunately – and I honestly do feel badly about this – that very night the young music student had arranged to give his first recital. A test piece by Schumann, at the Rudolf Steiner Hall.

I blame no one but myself. Even today, I still don't know whether it was the after-effect of the van man and me sitting so heavily on the frame of the harp to force the strings through the cheese; or whether it was just that cheese itself exerts some kind of emancipating effect upon harp-strings.

All that anyone knows for certain is, on the eighth bar of the

Schumann piece, when the young man from No. 14 grabbed a handful of strings and then, as is the way in harp-plucking, released them, they all flew out of the harp and struck a gentleman in the fourth row, a retired colonel who'd wandered in under the impression it was going to be that lecture on 'How To Cure Stammering'.

It's not a sequence of circumstances of which I'm in any way proud. But if relating it has done nothing else, it may have helped clear matters up for those of you who still puzzle over the headline which appeared the following morning above *The Times* music critic's review of the performance:

'Harp Strings Hit Colonel In The Schumann Test.'

FMFMFMFMFMFMFMFMFMFM

'Old Soldiers Never Die'

Song. 1914–1918

THE other morning I was sitting over my breakfast egg – I hadn't finished my toast and marmalade and I didn't want my egg to get cold – when my wife suddenly said, 'Do you know what I was doing exactly ten years ago this morning?' I raced back down Memory Lane. It was empty.

'No, what?'

'I was sitting in the top room of a Genoese watch-tower in Corsica, writing postcards under an umbrella.'

She was right. As I retrieved the egg from beneath me and started digging into it, memory flooded back. Of course – the priest and the eggs!

Ten years ago we bought a sort of mediaeval potting-shed in the hill village of Monticello, which sits six hundred feet above the small port of Ile-Rousse. We went out and moved in exactly ten years ago, on Easter Monday.

In no time we had the place shipshape; fresh newspaper on the table; packing-case lined with straw for the children to sleep in; and our own bed made up in the little room across the bridge, which was the top part of an ancient watch-tower. Pleasantly fatigued after all that, we strolled across the square to the bar for a quick Casanis, a Corsican aperitif based upon, I think, torpedo fluid and marine varnish. The first sip had hardly started corroding the fillings before the bad news was broken to us.

It seems that you must never sleep in a house in Corsica before it has been blessed by a priest.

And, more than that, there must be coloured eggs in every room to be blessed.

And so the awful chain of events began. There was not an egg to be had in the village, brown, white or variegated, and the shops were shut for the holiday.

Things were getting a little desperate and I couldn't think what to do next, apart from shout at the children, when I noticed some vaguely egg-shaped pots lying about. They were about a foot high and made of dirty-white earthenware. Apparently the villagers filled them with soil and grew things in them, like geraniums and carrots. We bore six of these off to our place and set about getting some colour into them. We boiled up my wife's new blue dress in a bucket, steeped the pots in that and they came out quite a pleasant pale blue. We steeped the other three in hot beetroot juice and they took on a fine mauve tinge. We had our coloured eggs. Now for the priest.

The nearest priest lived in Ile-Rousse, which was down three miles of hairpin bends. I borrowed a car from the man next door and set off. It was one of those tiny Citroens which the French are so fond of; they are made of corrugated iron and cock a leg going round corners. As the layout inside the car was totally alien I decided not to risk using the engine and just gave the thing a shove, jumped in and coasted all the way down to the port.

By the time I had located the priest and persuaded the priest to come up to Monticello – a triumph of diplomacy; he was ninety-two and had earache – it was dark. And it began to rain. Now Mediterranean rain differs from British rain. You don't get it so regularly but when you do it is bigger, faster, wetter, and it bounces higher.

It was when we were in the car, with the stuff pounding down on the roof, that I realised that I had no idea how to put the car into motion. Starting the engine was simple enough, merely a matter of turning the key. But the gears . . .

Citroen 2CVs don't go in for a gear-lever, as one understands a gear-lever. Instead, there is a white toffee-apple sticking out of the dashboard. And there is no indication anywhere as to which way the thing has to be turned, bent, lifted, pulled, inclined or thrust in order to locate first gear.

I wrestled with the toffee-apple for quite a long while, with the priest sitting quietly beside me mumbling to himself in Latin, when suddenly we lurched backwards. I had found reverse.

I resolved not to push my luck any farther, and backed gently towards Monticello.

All went well within the street lights of Ile-Rousse but once we had started reversing up the steep, twisted road to Monticello two things became apparent: a car's headlamps point forwards not backwards, and although windscreen wipers keep a driver's vision clear in the

39

heaviest of rain there are no windscreen wipers on the rear window.

There was nothing for it but to ask the priest to get out and walk ahead of the car to guide me.

It took us nearly an hour to climb the hill and I must say that it was a very tired, sodden and cross priest indeed who allowed me to propel him into our residence.

'There you are, Father,' I said, with a sweep of the hand. 'Coloured eggs as per instructions. Bless this house.'

But something had gone wrong. The 'eggs' were no longer coloured. In the two hours I had been absent the colour had completely faded from them and they were clearly just six earthenware pots, albeit egg-shaped.

'Ostrich eggs, Father,' I mumbled, without hope. 'Colouring very pale . . .'

He broke into words. 'These are not coloured eggs. These are jars which the villagers fill with soil to grow things like bougainvillea and turnips.'

'Now you come to mention it, Father,' I cried, fighting to the last, 'they DO look like jars used for growing things in. A fantastic resemblance . . .'

It was no use, of course. He wasn't fooled for a second by our anæmic pottery. The last we saw of him was his frail figure making for the bar.

So our house was not blessed.

And during the night a wind rose up and stripped half the tiles from the tower roof. And the rain continued to rain.

And next morning, when my wife wrote her postcards home, she had to do so sitting in the tower under an umbrella.

The irony is that I would never have made such a pathetic attempt to deceive the old priest if I had known then, as I know now, an ancient Corsican proverb:

'Old soil-jars never dye.'

DNDNDNDNDNDNDNDNDN

'Forever Amber'

Title of Novel
Kathleen Winsor

ONCE in a lifetime, every scriptwriter gets an idea that really fires him. In my case, from every film-studio that I've approached with it. But this idea, I pledge you, this is a blockbuster, it's the big one. What makes me so sure is – and isn't this always the real test? – I can outline the whole idea in just five words. Three, if hyphens count. A peace-time war-film!

What do you mean impossible? Will you just *listen*!

When you get right down to it, what is a war-film? Isn't the story always the same one? Some kind of mixed group – a fighter squadron, say, a commando platoon, a squad of marines, doesn't matter – an assemblage of individuals from all walks of life who finally, under the stress of combat and danger, learn how to work together as one unit? Right. So here's what we do. We take a peace-time equivalent of that kind of group and – now follow me here – we tell their story in exactly the same kind of terms.

I know what's going through your mind. What kind of peace-time group in any way resembles a group of war-time commandos, marines, fighter pilots? Okay, try this on for size. A Formation Dancing Team?

Suddenly gone quiet, haven't you? So let me fill the story in, just broad brush-strokes.

We open, like all those war-films do, at the place where 'it all happened'. But – as the place looks *now*, present day. Abandoned, empty, deserted. In our case, it's a ballroom. An abandoned, empty, deserted ballroom.

Into it wanders our hero. No longer a young man. Touches of grey here and there. But still looking good, of course. Sexy. Slowly he walks across the empty ballroom – we do the echo-thing with his footsteps – then he pauses. Looking down at the maple dance-floor, he rubs his

41

shoe on its dust. As the camera moves in on his face, into his eyes comes that look that tells us he's going to have a flashback. Far-off sounds creep in! Shuffle of patent-leather shoes, rustle of taffeta dresses, chickychickybomchick of a samba. As they get louder, louder, the whole screen goes sort of ripple-y – and when it clears up again, boom, we're in.

It's ten years ago – and there they are. The Mrs Eva Swaythling Formation Dancing Team. Six men, six women. The Clean Dozen. Heading them up – the Skipper. Mrs Eva Swaythling herself! Hard-bitten, loud-mouthed, ruthless. Joan Crawford if we can get her, if not we go for Charles Bronson.

She's barking out orders. 'I'm going to make dancers out of you if it means you rhumba on the stumps of your ankles!' Tough as they come, see? But, underneath it all, deep down – golden syrup.

Cut to cameos of each of the team. John Mills, the spoilt rich kid who finally learns humility. Richard Attenborough, the lovable cockney. ('Time for a brew-up, Skipper?') Sarah Miles, whose puppy is dying and medical science is baffled. The coloured boy, you can do this now, the coloured boy who turns out braver than anybody. Susan George, who gets raped by a second-trumpet player, but off-screen so we keep the U Certificate.

The Mrs Eva Swaythling Formation Dancers. . . . We do a mon-tage of their training. Mile after mile in quickstep tempo, carrying 250 lb of sequins on their backs. The pitiful shortage of equipment. 'How are we gonna get the material for the girls' dresses, Skip . . .?' 'Give us the tulle and we'll finish the job.'

Their first night-op. The Hammersmith Palais during a power-cut. We show their triumphs, we show their reverses. And not only their reverses, their chassis-turns, their scissors-steps. And always, right out there in front, Mrs Eva Swaythling. Threatening, cajoling, exhorting, 'There are no atheists in a foxtrot.'

Finally comes the this-is-the-moment-that-all-your-training's-been-the-preparation-for moment. They're going in against Jerry. It's the Eurovision Area Championships.

They're in the dressing room of the Streatham Locarno. Waiting. 'It's quiet out there. . . .' 'Too damned quiet. I don't like it. . . .' 'Time for a brew-up, Skipper?'

Crash of sound – and they're plunged into the maelstrom! Into the shrieking, pounding bombardment that is the Ken Mackintosh Orchestra. Thrills! Spills! Chills! In the fourth sequence of the

Military Two-Step, the Number Three man suddenly staggers. His shoe lace has snapped! But, like a well-oiled machine, the two girls either side of him move in and, without breaking step, support him between their puff-sleeves. He finishes the flower-pattern on one shoe!

It looks like nothing can stop them. But then, just as the Latin American heat starts – tragedy! Mrs Eva Swaythling winces, claps her hands to that iron bosom. Her face contorts. The Souvenir Brochure slips from her nerveless fingers. . . .

Around the ballroom the word flashes. 'Mrs Eva Swaythling's bought it!' In that great dance hall in the sky, there'll be a new pair of silver shoes tonight.

Momentarily the Team falter, become ragged. But it is the coloured boy who rallies them. 'Okay, gang. Let's get this one for the Skipper!'

The ballroom will never see Formation Dancing like that again. And, as the samba chickychickyboms to its climax, the Mrs Eva Swaythling Team realise they've done it. They've brought the Common Market Latin American Area Trophy back to Britain. . . .

Must be a milestone in screen history. Eh? Must be. There's only one thing that's still holding me up on it, apart from the fact that everyone thinks it's rotten. Finding the right title for it. *In Which We Swerve?* . . . *Last Military Two-Step In Streatham?* . . . Nuh.

No, I think there's only one title that captures the sweep and majesty of the story – that broken rallying-cry which snatched victory from the jaws of Latin American defeat. How does this grab you? . . .

'For Eva – Samba!'

FMFMFMFMFMFMFMFMFM

'Supercalifragilisticexpialidocious'

Title of song from 'Mary Poppins'

THE pure unalloyed joy, the flight of the heart on wings of song, the flowering of the spirit like the opening of a jacaranda-tree blossom at the prospect of my wife returning tomorrow after a week away is tempered by the thought of the squalid state the kitchen is in.

In order to preserve the balance of nature it is vital that I maintain the fiction that I am capable, at a pinch, of looking after myself and can be left for a few hours without change and decay taking over the household.

So, in the few hours left me, I have an alarming number of important things to do, most of which have been brought about by my firm conviction that women run things on old-fashioned, traditional lines which would benefit from the application of a cold, rational, male intelligence; i.e. mine.

First of all I must replenish the stock of tinned soup in the store cupboard. Round about Day Two I realised that man could live on tinned soup alone. It heats up in a jiffy and, more than that, the tin can be used as a throwaway saucepan. With the help of a pair of pliers to hold the thing, the empty tin can be used to boil eggs or anything else and then thrown away; the soul-numbing process of washing-up is thereby minimised. The trouble is that a keen female eye, viewing the stock cupboard, will spot at a glance that a suspicious quantity of tinned soup has been consumed. So it must be replaced.

On Day One I had realised that, as master of all I surveyed, I did not have to eat vegetables. I have no religious or moral objections to vegetables but they are, as it were, dull. They are the also-rans of the plate. One takes an egg, or a piece of meat, or fish, with pleasure but then one has, as a kind of penance, to dilute one's pleasure with a damp lump of boskage. However, this puritan attitude that no meal is worthy without veg. is strongly held in this house so I must somehow give the impression that vegetables have been consumed in quantity. What I must do is to buy a cauliflower and shake it about a bit in the kitchen. Fragments will then be found under the table and in corners, giving the impression that vegetables have been in the forefront of my diet.

And then there is the refrigerator. This seemed to me a most in-efficient instrument, yielding up stiff butter when I wanted it to spread, ice-cold milk when I wanted milk to warm up for the coffee, and when I needed some ice cubes the ice container was apparently welded to the shelf with cold. So I instituted a system whereby I switched off the fridge at breakfast, thereby making the contents malleable when I needed them, and switched it on again at night. This has worked quite well except that the contents of the fridge are now a cluster of variously-sized rectangular snowballs. I must remember to take a hammer and chisel to them before tomorrow.

And I need a stout elastic band because I have done in the vacuum cleaner. I used one of my gumboots for kitchen refuse to save messing about with a bin but liquids seeped through a hole in the toe. The obvious solution to a hole in a gumboot toe is to bung it up with a mixture of sawdust and the remains of that tin of car undersealing compound which one has in one's garage. I poured the underseal and the sawdust into a thing called a Liquidiser, which is a kind of electric food-mixer, but what I failed to note was that one is supposed to put the lid on before operating it. And when I began to vacuum clean the mixture of tar and sawdust off the kitchen ceiling it seemed to jam up the works. The motor went on running but there was a smell of burn-ing rubber and now I must, before tomorrow, provide the vacuum cleaner with a new rubber band.

And eggs. We have an ark in the orchard containing nine hens, which provide us with a regular intake of beige eggs. I went out to feed them on Evening One and I think that they missed my wife. They greeted me, I felt, reproachfully, making sounds not unlike those made by Mr Frankie Howerd. 'Ooh!' they went, 'Ooooh, OoooOOOh.' So I undid the door of the ark and led them on an educational tour of the garden, pointing out where the new drainage is to be laid, the place on the lawn where I had lost my lighter, the vulgar shape which one of the poplar trees had grown into. And then the dogs joined us and helped to take the chickens out of themselves by chasing them, and soon the air was filled with feathers and joyous squawks. I finally got the chickens back into the ark by midnight but, oddly, they haven't laid an egg between them the whole week. Since my wife will be expecting to be greeted by about three dozen beige eggs, I must do something about this before she returns.

I also had a spot of bother with a packet of frozen peas. I thought I would vary my diet by making myself a Spanish omelette, i.e. as I understood it, an omelette with a pea or two in it. Now the packet stated clearly that if less than four servings was required the necessary amount could be obtained by giving the frozen pack a sharp buffet with an instrument. I had my soup tin on the gas-stove, with a knob of butter in it, and I obeyed the instructions; that is to say, I held the frozen lump in my left hand and aimed a blow at it with a convenient instrument – my dog's drinking bowl. It worked up to a point. One frozen pea detached itself, bounced off my knee, and disappeared. Where had it gone? My Afghan hound was right next to me at the time, watching keenly what I was doing with her bowl, and I had a sudden horrible suspicion that the pea had gone into her ear. I called to her. She evinced no interest. I went round the other side and called again. She looked up. I made a mental note to take the dog to the vet for a swift peaectomy operation before tomorrow.

Lastly there is the problem of my breath. Last night I made myself a casserole of sausages – or rather, a soup-tin-role of sausages – but I seemed to have lost the salt. After a deal of searching I found an alien-looking container marked 'Sel' and applied it liberally. It seems that it was garlic salt. I did not realise what it had done to my breath – one doesn't with garlic – until this afternoon when I stood waiting for somebody to open a door to me and suddenly noticed that the varnish on the door was bubbling.

So I have a number of things to remember to do before tomorrow, such as tinned soup, a cauliflower, de-frosting the refrigerator, buying an elastic band for the vacuum-cleaner, getting in three dozen beige eggs, seeing the vet about the pea in the dog's ear and taking something for the garlic on my breath.

How, you are perhaps asking yourself, will he possibly remember all these things?

Well, hopefully I have put them all together into a kind of chant, or song. It goes:

'Soup . . . a cauli . . . fridge . . . elastic . . . eggs . . . pea . . . halitosis.'

DNDNDNDNDNDNDNDNDNDN

'Great Expectations'

Title of Novel
Charles Dickens

F it's true that we laugh loudest at that which we hate most, then
my favourite joke is the one that Ronnie Scott tells about the
fellow who says to a girl 'Do you like Dickens?' and she says 'I
don't know, I've never been to one.' Because I just can't be doing
with Dickens. It's some kind of blind spot, I'm sorry, he holds
out nothing whatever for me. That's why, if it hadn't been for a story
in this morning's newspaper, the above quotation would have put
me in a right hiatus.

It was a story about smuggling immigrants into Britain. As you
must know by now, there is, in this ancient seat of freedom, a growing
body of organised apoplexy which refuses to believe that immigration
is the sincerest form of flattery. Consequently, a minor but lucrative
hustle has grown up, based on smuggling persons of foreign origin
across our frontiers at a hundred and fifty pounds a nob.

Well, according to the newspaper story, one clever youngster hit on
a bright variation. He loaded sixteen Asian nationals inside a large
wooden crate, drilled the necessary air-holes, then had the crate flown
Air Freight to Heathrow. The intention was that once a lorry had off-
loaded it into the Freight Shed, he would then, prior to Customs
inspection, prise open the crate and assist its occupants to effect a
stealthy exit through the Spectators' Car Park.

And had it not been for the uncertain state of industrial relations at
London Airport, it would have made an exemplary essay in Creative
Smuggling. The crate was off-loaded from the plane, all right. But
just as the lorry was about to take it to the Freight Shed, a twenty-four-
hour strike was called.

The driver slammed on his brakes, switched off the ignition, climbed
out of his cab and scampered off to join his colleagues harmonising
'We Shall Not Be Moved' hard by the Departure Lounge. In conse-

quence, the crate of sixteen Asians was left at the far end of the runway until such time as the twenty-four-hour strike finished.

Well, another fact of life that will not have escaped you is that, in this country, the twenty-four-hour strike is like the twenty-four-hour 'flu. You have to reckon on it lasting at least five days.

This proved about three days too many for the crated Asians. On the second day, they held a whispered consultation. That, in itself, is no easy task when you're packed in layers of four. By a show of hands – again, not easy – they agreed that further confinement might prove too irksome to endure. So, using a system of co-ordinated inhaling and exhaling, they burst open the sides of the crate.

Too bad, really. They were immediately apprehended by the Chairman of BOAC. It just so happened he was taking a stroll out to the far end of the runway to try to get away from the sound of Clive Jenkins' voice.

Sad, isn't it, typical of the times in which we live, all goes to show, etc., etc.

Far as I'm concerned, though, if it hadn't been for the Heathrow Sixteen's resentment of their prolonged incarceration, I'd never have found that newspaper sub-head which circumvented my Dickensian block:

'Crate Irks Packed Asians.'

FMFMFMFMFMFMFMFMFM

'Ta-ra-ra-boom-de-ay!'

Title of song

I PROPOSE to tell you pretty well all there is to know about an animal which is very popular among dog-lovers though less so among dog-haters. I refer to the dog. Dogs, like horses, are quadrupeds. That is to say, they have four rupeds, one at each corner, on which they walk. In many other ways dogs are like horses – for example, they both like eating biscuits and being photographed and being tickled behind the ear – but they are not all THAT much like horses because they are smaller. Except, of course, if you match a very huge dog indeed up against a tiny, tiny horse who hasn't been well, when it is quite difficult to tell the difference between them.

If you find yourself in the predicament of facing a very large dog and a tiny horse, not knowing which is which, the wisest thing to do is to wait until they are both moving towards you then shout 'whoa!' The one that doesn't stop is the dog. This is a reasonably safe test unless the name of the horse is Woe, in which case they will both approach. Or the horse is deaf.

Dogs are very historical, some of the earliest being found by Marco Polo up Chinese mandarins' sleeves.

The Romans had dogs and named the Canary Islands after them, although this was by way of being a bit of a mistake: the Romans had very, very large and hairy canaries and very, very small yellow dogs and they got the two mixed up.

Much mention is made of dogs in English literature. The popular dog's name, Prince, comes from Shakespeare's *Hamlet*, where Prince was a Great Dane. From the same play comes a popular doggy expression 'Down, Prince!' uttered by Ophelia.

Another reference occurs in *Macbeth*. A dog misbehaves himself in the castle and Lady Macbeth, very cross, cries 'Out, damned Spot!'

Keats mentions a dog in one of his longer poems but I can't remember which one.

Elizabeth Barrett Browning had a King Charles spaniel which sat on the end of the sofa with her and helped her pine for Robert Browning but it did not have a memorable name.

Bill somebody-or-other in a novel by Charles Dickens had some sort of dog – I think it was a black-and-white one – but I've forgotten its name.

That is all I remember about dogs in English literature.

There is a large selection of various sorts of dogs for those interested in acquiring one. Poodles are very popular because they do not moult, or run amok and get their names in the paper, and they would much rather be people than dogs so – except twice a year – they do not bother much with each other. Poodles usually come in three shades, black, white and brown, though not all at once. Black ones are nice in that they don't show the dirt but when they sit down in the shadows they are invisible and you tend to tread on one by accident causing you to pitch forward, graze your knee on the radiator and end up with your elbow in the potatoes.

The Chow is a large, hairy dog with eyes rather like raisins and a mauve tongue which is the same mauve as that wine-gum which when you come to it you cover with your thumb and stop handing them round. They are very popular in Italy where a song was written to a Chow puppy: 'Chow, Chow, Bambino'.

Another large dog is the Afghan Hound, which looks like a greyhound in a fun-fur. Afghans are very beautiful. They eat meat, biscuits, fish, books, chairs, bicycle tyres, mattresses, carpets, tables, raincoats, trees, car upholstery and milkmen.

Greyhounds were once much more popular than they are nowadays, perhaps because they need so much exercising. Very few men are willing, after a hard day at the factory bench or in the boardroom, to arrive home and then take the greyhound out for its run, and many middle-aged men find it increasingly difficult to squeeze themselves into the trap.

Flat-dwellers in the modern world are turning increasingly towards smaller dogs and small dogs are becoming extremely popular. The smallest of all is the Chihuahua, a naked Mexican animal the size of a pound of stewing steak.

Not surprisingly, the Chihuahua is supplanting the bigger dogs in the affections of pet-owners. It is very difficult indeed to mistake a

Chihuahua for a horse. It requires very little exercise – a swift daily trot round the back-door mat suffices – and it could live happily in a telephone-box let alone a small flat. So no wonder the latest copy of the trade journal, *The Doggy Times*, carried a banner headline: 'Chihuahua Boom Today.'

DNDNDNDNDNDNDNDNDNDNDN

Now is the time for all good men to
come to the aid of the party

Edwin Meade Robinson
'The Typewriter's Song'

FOR the thinking man, there is much to be learned from that
piece of advice printed on most bottles of patent medicine:
'Keep Away from Small Children'. Personally, I've always
avoided them as much as possible. However, when the child is
your own and it's her fifth birthday party. . . .

It was an illuminating experience, if repulsive. One moment a tiny
shy thing, in her party dress, had her hand in mine, waiting for the
first of her little friends to arrive. A ring at the front door – then this
bulldozer hurled past me, wrenched the door open and with a 'Where's
my present, where's my present?' shoved the small guest up against a
wall and frisked him from head to foot. It is something of a jarring
moment when you realise you have brought another Customs Officer
into the world.

'She's over-excited,' I muttered to the boy's mother. But that lady's
gaze had already swept past what was going on in the hall and was
busy in the kitchen, pricing our units.

Ten minutes later there were twenty-three guests present. I spent
quite a while watching the little boys at play. What I found interesting was not so much that early defining of sexual roles about
which there's so much chat-show chatter these days, more how the
actual playing of the role has altered since my time. When I was that
age, small boys used to point pistols and say, 'Bang, bang, you're
dead.' Now they point pieces of plastic and say, 'Zap, zap, you're
sterile.'

While I was having a ponder on that, I felt a tug at my trousers. It
was one of the little girls. 'I'm Caroline.'

'I know, dear. So's practically everybody.'

We had eight Carolines present. Eight Carolines, five Rebeccas,
four Jakes and about half a dozen Jamies. Where have all the Harolds

52

and Muriels gone? Who was the last child to be christened Sadie? Caroline said, 'Do you like my new dress?'

'It's lovely, dear.'

'I'm wearing a bra.'

True as I'm sitting here. Didn't come up as far as my knee-cap. Don't you find something chilling about someone wearing uplift before they've got any up to lift? I had the greatest difficulty, the rest of the afternoon, restraining her from showing it to me.

Her persistence was only diverted by the announcement that tea was to be served. The tea also proved to be what Jimmy Durante used to call a revolting development. Talk about eat, drink and be messy. Has science ever explained why, at that age, the only time they sneeze is when they've just taken a mouthful of sponge cake?

But it was after the meal that the really interesting problem arose. There is one lesson to be drawn from it that I can pass on to you immediately. When giving children's parties, never serve eight jugs of orangeade in a house which has only one bathroom. What you are immediately brought up against is the myth that the British are united by a common language. It was one of the Simons who came up to me first. 'Mister,' he said, 'I want to go soo-soo.'

I narrowed my eyes at him. 'You want to what?' But the fattest of the Rebeccas was now pulling my sleeve. 'Yes, dear?'

'Where do I tinkle?' she said. As I stared at her blankly, a rather red-faced Jake came dashing in. Very fast. 'Make whistle-whistle,' he announced. Urgently.

'Look, children,' I began – but, at that moment, the most soignee of the Carolines entered the room. 'I want to go to the loo,' she said.

The penny dropped. I turned back to the original Simon, the one who'd uttered the first request. 'Hear that, lad?' I asked him. 'That's what you should have said. "I want to go to the loo."'

'Not any more,' he said.

What has the education explosion really achieved, I wondered to myself later that evening as I was rubbing away at the carpet. What kind of society is it where parents have narrowed the range of names which their children can be christened down to little more than half a dozen, while at the same time creating an infinity of names for the potty?

What's needed, I decided, is a standardisation of appellation in the second area. And it's needed right away, before we all disappear down the generation gap. What I suggest is a Royal Commission – headed, preferably, by someone of the stature of Lord Goodman – to decide on one official phrase to which everybody's children will then conform.

If you're with me on this, please send S.A.E. You will receive by return a sticker for the rear window of your car:

'Now Is The Time For Lord Goodman To Come To The Aid Of The Potty.'

FMFMFMFMFMFMFMFMFM

They bore him barefac'd on the bier

William Shakespeare. 'Hamlet', iv.v.

WONDER whether you share my delight in Fanny Hill? I find it really pretty there in the Spring, so easy to get to from Godalming by bicycle and there is a lovely view from the top if you stand on your saddle. I was doing just that some five years ago when I detected that something was amiss. 'Hello, Frank,' I distinctly remember saying to myself as I balanced precariously with one foot on the saddle, 'all is not A.1 at Lloyd's.'

The reason for my perturbation was that I seemed not to be seeing quite as much of the lovely countryside as I was accustomed to see: the lady who took her Sunday afternoon bath at exactly four o'clock in the small cottage two hundred yards beyond the hedge was still visible. But only from the neck up.

I pondered. Either the thicket hedge had grown sharply since the previous Sunday thus cutting off the view, or I had sunk slightly.

I checked. Bicycle against the same telegraph pole. Same shoes. Socks no thinner; the same hand-knitted heather mixture. Then I saw. My rear tyre was quite flat. I had a puncture.

No problem, of course, to a practical man. I levered the tyre off with the tablespoon I always carry with me for my hourly spoonful of Queen Bee honey, licked round the inner-tube until I detected the bubble and started to apply the tube of sticky stuff. Then happened what frequently happens when, for instance, one is faced with a particularly intricate crossword puzzle clue – the solution did not immediately present itself. I squeezed the tube, jumped on it and bit it but it was hopeless; the stuff inside had perished. I resolved to seek help. Lying some way back from the road was a house I had often noticed when I was idly waiting for four o'clock to arrive; an odd Victorian gothic residence set about with fruit trees and a croquet lawn.

55

The door was opened by a prim, middle-aged maid, clad in the uniform of her kind. She dropped a little, old-fashioned curtsey and murmured that she would inform the master. As I waited in the hall, contemplating the mezzo-tints of past-Presidents of the Royal Philanthropic Society, my mind was troubled. There was something about the maid that was curious, unusual. But what? 'Come along, Frank,' I remember saying to myself, 'there's something about her that's not all tickety-boo.' Then I realised what it was. She had a vast spade beard.

At that moment another woman, visibly the housekeeper, came in to say that Mr Pennithorne Phipps would see me. She was middle-aged, dressed in black, and her beard, though luxuriant, was a faintly fictional shade of auburn. Perhaps – who knows a woman's wiles – aided by a dab from a bottle?

Mr Pennithorne Phipps, a kindly, elderly man, received me affably, gave me a tube of rubber solution and a glass of cloudy sherry and insisted on telling me his story.

As a comparatively young man he had inherited a large sum of money which he resolved to put to some good purpose. A close friend, after trying unsuccessfully to sell him a gold-mine in Basingstoke, reluctantly accepted this philanthropic intent and advised him to do what he could to alleviate the plight of circus folk, who were being put out of work in their thousands due to people being more interested in the wireless and the cinema than in going to the circus.

Young Pennithorne Phipps set to with a will, which had been through Probate and had made him a very rich man indeed. He persuaded motor-car manufacturers to hire the India-Rubber Men to demonstrate how simple it was to get in and out of their smaller cars. He talked restaurateurs into engaging the Lilliputian Midgets to sit in their restaurants and so make the servings look bigger. He hired the Human Cannonballs to seaside landladies – after the flight was timed the landlady could legally advertise 'Only one minute from the sea'.

But he could find no work for four bearded ladies. They were shy of other people. It was obviously too dangerous for them to go into industry and have to bend over lathes or sewing-machines. Their chances of a modelling career were slim. So he decided to take them into his house to look after him. And this they did most delightfully, one gardening, one cooking, one housekeeping, and one maiding. And in the long winter evenings, when the shadows drew in, they would plait each other's beards with pale ribbons on the ends of which were little wooden balls. Then the four of them would bend over their dulcimers and, with little twitches and nods of their heads, play for him the airs he never tired of hearing, like Corelli's Concerto Grosso in G Minor, and 'Put A Bit Of Powder On It, Father'. And when he was down in the dumps and *triste* they would amuse him by playing Beard Football, which was like Blow Football but instead of blowing down tubes to urge the ball into the goal the ladies tried to sweep it in with their beards.

That was five years ago. I never returned to the house, nor to the hill, because of a serious accident which befell me a few minutes after leaving the house. I mended my puncture and took up my usual position on tiptoe on the saddle, observing the scenery. All was as usual. The lady enjoyed her bath, as did I, until, quite unexpectedly, the lady did something most imaginative with her loofah and I fell off the bike.

The hospital did what they could but it was a complicated fracture. 'Give it to me straight, Doctor,' I said. She paused for a moment, then said, 'I live in a cottage about two hundred yards from a hill – you won't have heard of it – Fanny Hill. It's only a weekend cottage – I go there for a rest, and a bath, on Sundays – but I love that little hill. I'm sorry . . . but you will never be able to cycle up any sort of hill again.'

Nor have I. But last week a friend lent me his light van for the week-end and I had a sudden urge to recapture the pleasures of those Sundays five years ago. I drove to Fanny Hill. As I had ten minutes in hand before four o'clock I, on an impulse, called at the old Victorian gothic cottage.

What a change I found. The door was opened by the same maid – but she was clean shaven, and she smelt very strongly of brown ale.

'Dunno where he is,' she said, and left me.

I glanced behind me. The lawns were lumpy and the croquet hoops were mottled with rust.

A noise made me turn back. It was the housekeeper descending the stairs; the last two on her behind.

'Hang on, cock,' she said, 'I'll fetch the old fool.'

She, too, was clean shaven.

It was a sad Pennithorne Phipps indeed who faced me. It seems that he grew troubled about his four bearded ladies shortly after I had last seen them. Although they were entirely content he felt that perhaps he was being selfish in keeping them within the confines of the house. So he brought a specialist man down from London and paid for him to remove their beards by electrolysis. They were now normal women, able to take their place in society.

'It's been frightful,' he said. 'They troop down to the village every evening; they spend most of the time in the pub downing gallons of brown ale . . . there's no dulcimer playing . . . they can't now . . . nor Beard Football . . . instead of being happy, perfectly adjusted people they have become quarrelsome, competitive and, well, just plain dreary. They are now very dull people indeed.'

A few minutes later, as I took my aluminium ladder from the back of the van, adjusted it against the telegraph pole, got myself comfortably into position, binoculars at the ready, I thought over the sad story of Pennithorne Phipps and it seemed to contain a moral: Kindness is a lovely thing, but too much kindness can, in a funny way, corrupt.

Poor Pennithorne Phipps's ladies. Bearded and out of the ordinary, they were delightful people. But now . . .

They bore him – bare-faced, on the beer.

DNDNDNDNDNDNDNDNDNDN

The least said, soonest mended

Charles Dickens
'The Pickwick Papers'

THIS is the phrase on which the Glastonberrys have based
their lawsuit against the ground-landlord. Tell you about
the Glastonberrys. They're our local monied couple. Rich,
rich, rich. Mr Glastonberry has some sort of corner in flag-
pole manufacturing, a small-boned man whose life seems
dedicated to the proposition that Neatness Counts. He always looks
so exceptionally dapper, the local theory is that she keeps a plastic
cover over him when not in use. Mrs Glastonberry is all Wedgewood
hair and lipstick on the teeth, the sort of woman who asks for the
wine-list in a Wimpy Bar.

Their passion is houses. They buy and discard houses as though on a
winning streak in Monopoly. Over the past ten years, they must have
lived in eight different houses, each one featuring some conspicuously
exotic adjunct of gracious living. One house had a conversation-pit,
another a barbecue-terrace. I can remember an indoor ski-slope, a set
of pornographic stained-glass windows, a pelota court. . . .

But it was the novelty-item in her latest home that brought on the
lawsuit. 'Do come and see our new pad,' she called to me in the
Washeteria soon after they moved in. 'We got it because of the sauna.'

That statement was true, as has since been revealed, in a very exact
sense. It was only by reason of the sauna that the house had come on the
market at all. The previous owner had perished in it.

Poor old soul, it was one of those chance-in-a-million situations. He'd
entered it – if you've never seen a sauna, it's like a sort of sweating-hot
garden-shed – he'd turned the temperature up to about 120 degrees,
lolled about till he was the colour of shrimp-cocktail, then gone to
open the door to go out for a cooling shower. The handle of the door
had jammed. . . .

I must say, when Mrs Glastonberry recounted this to me that

evening, my keenness to enter the sauna waned. 'Oh, it's in perfect working order now,' she assured me. 'The landlord's had it repaired. We made that a condition of the lease. But, anyway, Walter insists that he should be the first one to try it.'

Walter is the son. A somewhat unhealthily complexioned fifteen-year-old, who always puts me in mind of one of Krafft-Ebing's footnotes. What my Mother calls 'sly'.

He came bustling up with a towel round his middle. 'Mother,' he said, 'if we want to do this right, we've got to do it the Scandinavian way.'

'What's the Scandinavian way, dear?'

'Mixed.'

They have this au-pair girl called Gia. A rather striking-looking Italian, who walks as though she never exhales. Mrs Glastonberry looked disconcerted.

'Oh, Mum, don't be a wet. It's only ten minutes. For heaven's sake, if a thing's worth doing –'

Enter Gia wearing a towel that started late and finished early. Walter took her hand, and they entered the sauna. It's a converted cupboard under the stairs, really, which the poor old previous owner had lined with lead and had a special kind of stove put in.

We waited outside it, sipping drinks and munching squares of toast which had been smeared with foodstuffs of such unidentifiable blandness, they were a kind of gastronomic Muzak.

After about half an hour, uneasiness was noticeably prevalent. 'Are you all right in there, Walter?' Mrs Glastonberry called, tapping on the door with her solitaire.

'Mum, the handle's jammed again.'

Consternation. 'Harold,' said Mrs Glastonberry to her husband, 'your fifteen-year-old son is locked in there with a nude Italian!'

After some consideration, Harold said, 'And think of the heat.'

We tried opening the door from the outside. It rattled a bit but didn't budge. Five of us got our shoulders together and charged the door. Not a hope. Lead-lined, you see, for the insulation.

'Mum,' came Walter's voice, 'Gia's fainted.'

'Move to the far side of the sauna immediately,' said Mrs Glastonberry.

'Don't worry, Mum,' Walter said a moment later, 'I'm giving her the kiss of life.'

He continued giving it to her, according to my Timex, for the next hour and ahalf. At midnight, someone suggested we fetch the Vicar and try to persuade him to marry them through the keyhole.

Five minutes after that, the door opened and Walter and Gia emerged. They looked, as newspapers say, little the worse for their ordeal. Looked, in fact, all things considered, extraordinarily cheerful. Another note I made, but nobody else seemed to, was that on emerging Walter extracted a key from the inside of the door and slipped it under his towel.

It was when the Sicilian relatives started coming over for the wedding that the Glastonberrys instituted their lawsuit against the landlord for failing to carry out stipulated repairs. Personally, I think they've got a good case. After all, as Mrs Glastonberry keeps trying to translate into Italian:

'The lease said sauna's mended.'

FMFMFMFMFMFMFMFMFM

Ring down the curtain, the farce is over

Rabelais's last words (attributed)

I WAS in the morning room. I shouldn't have been in the morning room because it was half-past two in the afternoon, but I couldn't go into the sitting room because I wanted to stand. Or, to be more accurate, I wanted to walk. And the sitting room is hardly the place in which to walk, let alone stand.

It was my desire to walk backwards and forwards. I much prefer walking backwards and forwards because it saves turning. I walk forward as far as I can go – usually until the tip of my nose comes to rest against the wallpaper – and then I walk backwards as far as I can go – usually indicated by the back of my head gently bumping against the wall. I then proceed forward again and repeat the process until I have walked enough.

If, on the other hand, I turned when I reached the wall rather than reversing, then this would mean that the sole of my right shoe would wear out more quickly than that of the left – I find that I usually turn on my right foot – which would lead to difficulties when the right shoe became due for repair at a time when the left shoe was still serviceable.

The need to reverse rather than turn was further strengthened by the fact that I was carrying an anvil in my right hand. The weight of this would have considerably accelerated the wear on the sole of the right shoe.

I had passed a length of stout rope round the anvil, leaving a loop by which to carry the thing. It was this loop that I was holding by the right hand as I walked up and down the morning room that afternoon. I was carrying the anvil because I wished to make my right arm half an inch longer – I had bought an inexpensive tweed sports jacket the right arm of which was half an inch longer than the left.

After perhaps an hour of walking a friend of mine, a retired tee-planter – he used to be a golfer's caddy – came in to see me. They say that the definition of a friend is someone to whom you don't feel obliged to speak. My friend sat watching me for an hour in silence, and then left.

Shortly after that I heard my wife calling. I put down the anvil and made my way into the drawing room where I found my wife quietly drawing. She is quite artistic and has made a fine collection of English kitsch which she has on display in the kitchen.

'Yes, my love?' I began, when I suddenly noticed with mounting horror that neither of her feet was touching the ground.

I started forward, but a closer examination revealed that she was lying on the sofa.

'Why is there a hole through the drawing room wall just by your chair?' she asked. 'Did you make it?'

'Indeed I did!' I said warmly. 'With a hammer and a cold chisel only this very morning.'

'Why did you knock a hole through our drawing room wall?'

'Quite simply, my love, to enable me to play the bass flute should I ever wish to take it up. You will notice that my chair is hard up against the wall and that the wall is on the right of the chair. If the urge ever came upon me to learn to play the bass flute I now have enough room to the right of me – an essential prerequisite of bass flute-playing just as enough room in front is necessary to a trombonist.'

'Yes, but the wind blows straight through the hole and the rain comes in. Surely there is something you can put over the hole until you decide whether or not to take up the bass flute?'

'Good thinking, my dear,' I said. 'You know what would answer the purpose if we could lay our hands on one – a framed aquatint of Lowestoft Harbour showing the Old Groin.'

It took us days to find one.

Then in came this auction catalogue of the village roadsweeper's effects. He had won the pools and bought the Uffizi Palace in Florence so was selling off his former possessions in five lots, namely, lot one – a gas ring, circa 1952, with a faulty tube; lot two – a pile of down useful for stuffing pillows; lot three – a double-damask curtain of great age which did him in lieu of a front door; lot four – his sole article of furniture, a rickety Victorian sofa covered with carved squiggles and ornaments; and lot five – a framed aquatint of Lowestoft Harbour showing the Old Groin.

I hurried round to the auction-room with a feeling that destiny was

63

on my side. The man there said that lot five would come up at about a quarter to four, so I was in plenty of time.

Bidding started briskly for the gas ring. It had reached 5p when I thought I had better check the time. Now I wear my watch on my right wrist to confuse thieves and I was wearing my new, inexpensive sports jacket with the overlong sleeve. I put my arm up and wriggled it so that I could read the time on my watch and found that I had bought the gas ring.

This was most vexing. But even more vexing was that exactly the same thing happened with the pile of down, the double-damask curtain and the fussy Victorian settee. And when the auctioneer did get to lot five – the aquatint – I had no money left to buy it.

I trailed miserably home and found my wife busy doing some sums in the summerhouse.

'Well?' she said, eagerly. 'Did you bid?'

'I did,' I replied.

'And did you buy it?'

'I bought,' I said, picking my words carefully. 'But not it.'

'Now look here, Rover,' said my wife, using the pet name she always applies in moments of anger, 'just what have you bought?'

In a very small voice I whispered:

'Ring . . . down . . . the curtain . . . the fussy sofa.'

DNDNDNDNDNDNDNDNDNDN

His word is as good as his bond

Proverb
Seventeenth century

FULL-FRONTAL nudity – and there's as catch-penny an opening as you'll ever see – has now become accepted by every branch of the theatrical profession with the possible exception of lady accordion-players. There is, however, one group of performers whom it threatens to relegate to the status of an endangered species. Conjurors.

It takes but a moment's reflection to realise why. Think of all those live doves, lighted cigarettes, steel rings. Where, with no clothes to secrete them *in*, is a conjuror to produce them *from*? A naked conjuror is at as much of a disadvantage as a vegetarian vampire or a cautious lemming.

That's why my heart went out to Nigel Gascoyne, Society Illusionist. Particularly as he was already under a bit of a cloud, following an unfortunate lapse of concentration during his 'Sawing A Woman In Half' illusion. 'Oh, it's a swine of a trick, that is,' he confided to me afterwards, 'if you allow your mind to wander for even a *second* . . .' Fortunately, the mishap didn't prove fatal and the lady concerned is now living contentedly in Scarborough. And Devon.

But the ensuing publicity, coupled with the growing public hunger for more and more nudity in entertainment, meant hard times for Nigel. From the elegant purlieus of London's glittering West End, he was reduced to performing in cheap Holiday camps, convalescent homes for the more obscure diseases, TUC Conferences . . .

'You just got to find a way of sexing-up the act, Nige,' his agent kept saying. 'It's flesh they want these days.'

'From a *conjuror*?' Nigel said bleakly.

But remonstrance was futile. The downward drift continued. Gradually he found himself performing to smaller and smaller audiences – The Clarence Hatry Dividend Club, the Vladivostok Young Conservatives, the ITA Opera Appreciation Society.... Piece by piece, he was reduced to selling-off his equipment, the very tools of his trade. The interlocking steel rings went to a scrap-metal merchant, the doves to a pacifist rally, the fifteen tied-together multi-coloured silk handkerchiefs to a Property Developer with hay-fever.

By Christmas Eve, all that remained of that rich diversity of exotica which Nigel had been wont to produce from about his person was one egg – a pathetic relic of his 'disappearing an egg from inside a black velvet bag' illusion. Oh, it had been a sensation in cabaret, that illusion. The awed murmurs that the egg's disappearance used to evoke from highly-placed executives at Management-By-Objective banquets! ('Surely he must be a devotee of witchcraft, a follower of the left-hand path?')

But life is not always a cabaret, old chum. Today that egg was all that stood between Nigel and starvation. Alone in his squalid bed-sit, he gazed at it, wishing there were only some way he could cook it. Oh, there was a gas ring by the grimy wall – but he no longer had the wherewithal to replenish its greedy slot. 'That's show-business, all right,' he reflected bitterly. 'When a 10p piece for the meter is beyond the means of someone whose very name is Gascoyne.'

Perhaps he could kindle a fire in the grate with his faded press-notices? But would they burn strongly enough to boil an egg? Probably not. Something more solid in the way of fuel was needed. A piece of wood of some kind? A piece of wood. ...

Can there be a more tragic symbol of surrender than a conjuror burning his wand? The wand, after all, is at the very heart of the conjuring experience. A wandless conjuror becomes, almost by definition, as incapable of function as a deaf lumberjack (can't hear TIMBER!) or a bow-legged wine-waiter (can't hold the bottle between knees for pulling cork out).

Or so one would have said. However, in a nearby room of that dingy lodging-house, crouched another practitioner of the performing arts: a former strip-tease artist named Alice B. Topless. She also had become a casualty to the sociological malaise which Veblen has called 'conspicuous display', but she preferred to describe as 'too much bleeding amateur competition'.

Now – alone, penniless, starving – she was contemplating putting an end to it all by impaling herself on a portable TV aerial. But as she moved towards it, she suddenly paused – sniffed. So sharpened by hunger had her senses become, her delicate nostrils had detected, drifting across that sordid hallway, the aroma of boiling egg! Timidly, she went out into the hall and tapped on Nigel's door . . .

Today 'Nigel Gascoyne & Alice – The Daring Deceivers' are a show business legend. Did I say a conjuror without a wand is incapable of functioning? That must now be qualified. What we failed to consider was the *purpose* of a wand. Why does a conjuror make such play with the wand when tapping it sharply against the rim of a black velvet bag? For only one reason: to draw your eyes away from what his other hand is groping for inside the recesses of his tail-coat. In other words, the wand is only there to 'misdirect', to distract the audience's attention.

Bearing that in mind, suppose now that, instead of a wand, your conjuror has an extremely beautiful bird standing at his side. And, at the point in the illusion when he wants all eyes diverted away from him – at that exact moment, every stitch of that bird's clothing *falls to the ground!*

All requirements are satisfied, aren't they? The moral seems to be that, these days, a nude lady-assistant can serve a conjuror's purposes every bit as effectively as his little bit of wood used to. Or, as Alice herself puts it:

'His bird is as good as his wand.'

The Law is not concerned with trifles

Old legal maxim

To His Honour, The Chief Judge,
The Centre Court,
Old Bailey,
London.

Dear Honour,

No doubt you wondered why I did not present myself, as the policeman told me to, at your court last Wednesday at 10.30 inst. to answer the charge which had been levelled at me, viz. and to wit as under. Namely, that I did heave, with malice aforethought, a quantity of hot food over the personages of Lord Ickenham, Lady Ickenham, the Hon. Ickenham and their three guests, causing them to sustain distress, a bill for dry-cleaning and, in the case of Lady Ickenham, half a pint of hot gravy down the cleavage.

The reason I did not turn up for my trial, Your Worship, lies in the circumstances as follows.

Until the day before the occurrence occurred I had been, by profession, unemployed. Then I saw this advertisement that a waiter was required for the restaurant up the Post Office Tower. Your Grace probably does not eat out much of an evening what with having to wear that wig and the funny clothes and being laughed at by other diners so I will fill you in a bit about the restaurant. It resides, as I said, five hundred and ninety feet up the Post Office Tower. It gives a pretty view over London and the menu is about four foot square.

I arrived for my appointment with the manager an hour and a half late and had to have a lie-down before he could ask me any questions (I have since learnt that it is possible to get to the top by lift), but he decided that as he was so short-handed he would give me a try-out and I was to start immediately.

What he forgot to tell me, what with me being late and lunch having started and the tables full of rich people looking out of the windows and saying 'That must be Highgate', was that the restaurant revolves.

This is a most important part of my case, Lord. I should have been told that the restaurant revolves. It is not – I maintain – a normal thing for a restaurant to do and unless one is given the nod beforehand one's natural expectancy is that the place will stay put.

How it works is like this. The whole thing is circular, that is to say, round. The kitchen and the Ladies and Gents and the wine cellar and so on are in the middle. In a sort of circular core. Round this is a perimeter, about twelve feet wide, on which are the tables. It is this outer ring, with the people on it, which revolves. It does not whizz round at a great lick, My Honour, or the eaters would be flung out of the windows and scattered all over Soho. It revolves very slowly so as you hardly notice. And I should have been told.

I emerged from the kitchen and at the first table in front of me was Lord Ickenham's party. I adjusted the carbon in my pad, briskly noted their first order, which was for soup, about-turned and walked straight into the Ladies. I covered up as best I could by mumbling 'Sorry gentlemen' and found my way back to the kitchen next door, but it was an unnerving experience; the two rooms seem to have changed places behind my back.

I put six bowls of soup on a tray and headed out again. But Lord Ickenham and party had apparently got fed up with waiting and left. At their table was a party of Japanese tourists. They did not want soup so I turned to go back to the kitchen and found myself in the manager's office. By now I was beginning to feel ill. I returned to the Japanese to find that they too had left and the table was now occupied by a jolly party from Uttoxeter who gave me a huge order for spaghetti and asparagus with butter sauce and roast beef and fish.

By this time I had realised that all was not what it seemed to be, so I walked very carefully through the door which I *knew* was the kitchen. It was the wine cellar. The kitchen proved to be right round the other side of the curved wall of doors. I loaded up my tray with the mass of food ordered by the Uttoxeter party and emerged cautiously from the kitchen. . . .

Imagine my surprise, and delight, to find sitting seated at the table in front of me my original party, consisting and comprising of Lord Ickenham, Lady Ickenham, the Hon. Ickenham and their three guests.

I was so pleased at things returning, as it were, to normal that I rushed forward to greet them, bearing the loaded tray above my head.

This, I now realise, was a mistake. For one thing it is never a good policy to rush forward bearing loaded trays. For another thing, there is a join where the bit which revolves meets the bit which stays put. Not a huge join, but just big enough a join for one's toe to catch in.

Suffice it to say, Your Lord, that I tripped and my whole trayful of hot nosh deluged Lord Ickenham and party – particularly Lady Ickenham.

Quite naturally I fled the scene. I rushed for the manager's office to offer him my personal resignation. But it was not the manager's office which I entered. Once again something had happened to the geography and what I entered was, in point of fact, the service lift. Or more precisely the service lift-shaft, the lift itself being at ground level at the time.

And that is why I was unable to be with you at the trial last Wednesday, and why I am writing this from my hospital bed. The surgeon said I was very lucky in that I fell on my head and I should be out and about again in a month or so. I will certainly pop in and see My Lordship when I am my old self again.

But in the interim I would like to point out, Worship, that I do not think that Lord Ickenham has a case. I am sure that I do not need to remind Thee of the rules which govern English Courts of Justice, and have done from time immoral. And I would bring to the court's notice that great maxim which is the cornerstone of British justice and jury's prudence:

The Law is not Concerned with Trayfulls.

Frank Muir

DNDNDNDNDNDNDNDNDNDN

Where there's a will, there's a way

G. Herbert (1640)
'Outlandish Proverbs'

HEN it finally became apparent that the entertainment business was the only career for which I was
suited – and that's quoting my Latin Master more or
less exactly – I went to a large cinema in Leicester
Square and pleaded with them to take me on, in any
capacity, however menial. The Manager said, 'The only vacancy I've
got is for an Ice Cream Girl.'

'Try me,' I said.

I can't say I enjoyed the experience. The shoulder-straps of those
trays are calibrated for feminine sizes, which meant I had to wear the
tray itself so high on my chest, I kept getting the orange-drink straws
up my nostril. So I was fairly relieved when the Manager told me I
was to be moved to another post.

'You wanted to start at the very bottom rung of the ladder?' he asked.
I nodded. He pointed towards something propped up against the
cinema canopy. 'There's the ladder.'

The new job was rather grandly titled 'Head of Display'. All it
really entailed was climbing up the ladder and affixing, high on the
front wall of the cinema, those four-foot-tall metal letters which spell
out the name of the film on that week.

I can't say it was a glamorous task. In a high wind, it was often dicey
and – artistically – it was something less than fulfilling. Unlike a
painter or a sculptor, I was in no position to step back and survey my
finished work. This led, in the first few weeks, to certain errors of
judgment, among which I can remember WEST SIDE SORTY, THE
SNOUD OF MUSIC and SANE CONNERY IN GLODFINGER.

Nevertheless, the work did make me feel that little bit nearer to the
great throbbing heart of show business. If it were not for me, I used to
think, as I surveyed the entertainment-hungry crowds milling around

Leicester Square, those people would have to make guesses at what we're showing tonight.

But it is only the moment of emergency which really transforms us into troupers. My moment came when the telephone rang at three o'clock one morning. It was the Manager. 'I just passed the cinema on my way home from a Ban The Pill meeting,' he said. 'Your Y has dropped off.'

Fuddled with sleep as I was, I immediately comprehended the urgency of his concern. The film we were showing that week was *My Fair Lady*. Although the new liberalisation of attitudes had begun to emerge and Gay Power was already nascent, it was still not yet on for a Leicester Square first-run house to appear to be exhibiting a film called MY FAIR LAD.

When my hastily-summoned taxi reached the cinema, I found the letter Y lying, twisted and splintered, on the pavement. Obviously, it was ruined beyond repair. I hastened to the store-room where the spare letters were kept. There was no spare Y!

Perhaps I can construct one, I thought. Attention was already beginning to be paid to John Schlesinger, Ken Russell and Sam Peckinpah, so we had no shortage of Xs in stock. Perhaps I could take an X and change it into a Y by just sawing off the, as it were, south-east leg?

No luck. I did it all right, but it wouldn't stay up on the wall. What to do? Where, in London, at four o'clock in the morning, can one lay hands on a four-foot-tall letter Y?

Well, if necessity is the mother of invention, there are times when it is also the mother-in-law. In other words, it can occasionally spur one to the kind of expedient which one would rather not think oneself capable of.

In my case, theft. From the cinema on the opposite side of Leicester Square, which was showing a film whose title contained the letter I wanted. As, at that time of the morning, people get up to all sorts of strange things in the West End, nobody even paused to stare when I shinned up the facia of that cinema and removed its enormous Y.

The only nasty moment came when I was carrying it across Coventry Street. A policeman stopped me – 'Excuse me, sir. What might you be doing walking along at 4.30 a.m. carrying a four-foot letter Y?'

Fortunately, I kept my presence of mind, or cool, as it was only just beginning to be called. 'This is not a letter Y, officer,' I said. 'I am an itinerant water-diviner. My preference happens to be for the larger-sized twig.'

He even touched his helmet to me as he went on his way. By 5 a.m., the fair name of *My Fair Lady* was restored. True, the cinema opposite, which had been packing them in with a magnificent John Huston classic starring Gregory Peck and Orson Welles, now appeared to be showing a film called MOB DICK. But that's, as I felt myself entitled to say for the very first time, show business.

I've had warm feelings towards the screen version of Herman Melville's great allegorical novel ever since. Indeed, I recommend that any other aspiring Head of Display who ever finds himself in a similar predicament to mine seek around for a cinema showing it. You'll find what I found:

Where there's a whale, there's a Y.

FMFMFMFMFMFMFMFMFMFM

My love is like a red, red rose

Robert Burns

ARE you there, Jimmy Young? You of the cheerful chatter and the gramophone records and the recipe of the day? I have been a staunch listener this many a year, Jimmy Young, and I have just tried out one of your recipes so I thought perhaps you might like to know how it turned out.

I did everything exactly as you said, picking up pad and pencil exactly when you told me to – I had to steer with my teeth – and I obeyed the recipe to the letter.

You do an awful lot of recipes, usually for strange delights like Savoury Baked-bean Meringues or Pilchard Tartlets, so you probably don't remember mine offhand – but it was for a Farmyard Cottage Loaf. Good, old-fashioned home-made bread.

You began by asking me to grab hold of two pounds of 'plain' flour. You kept repeating that it must be 'plain' flour but you didn't spell the word 'plain'. Well, Jim, I live quite near the airport so I dropped in on the way home. Do you know something? They don't bake on planes. Those ice-cold sandwiches they hand round are not made on board; the bread is baked on the ground. So I bought some flour which the grocer said was 'Self-raising'; it seemed the next best thing.

Then you said 'take a pint of water'. Bit of a problem there because the bathroom scales only work in stones and pounds. But I found a quart bottle, took this round to the pub and asked the barman to put a pint of draught in it. Once home I got a milk bottle of water and measured how much water I had to add to the beer to fill the bottle. I then emptied the bottle and poured in this same, measured, amount of water. The empty space in the bottle now represented exactly one pint. All I had to do then was fill the bottle and measure how much water it took and I had my pint. As a point of interest, Jim, a pint is roughly the amount contained in a small milk bottle.

Next you said salt – a pinch. No problem; the kitchen window next door was open.

Then came yeast – a lump the size of a walnut – which you said could be obtained from any Baker. I tooled straight round to my nearest Baker, Ernie Baker who mends bicycles, but he'd never heard of the stuff. Luckily I managed to pick up a knob from the cakeshop. It's a sort of yellow dough, Jim, and it stinks.

You then told me to put the flour, yeast, salt and water into a bowl, which I did. You then said that for twenty minutes it had to be kneaded. That was a tricky business, Jim, and I have a couple of hints which you might give your listeners if you repeat this recipe some time in the future. When kneading it is advisable to roll the trousers up first. If you forget to do this and you can't get the dough off with hot water or petrol quite a good tip is to burn the trousers. I found the most practical way of kneading was to divide the dough into two large bowls, put these on the floor and use one knee to each bowl, hanging on to the edge of the kitchen table for balance. Another advantage to this method is that if, as happened to me, the vicar calls in the middle of the process, you can make your way slowly to the front door, Toulouse-Lautrec style, without interrupting the process.

Your next instruction, Jim, was to find a warm place, about 80 degrees Fahrenheit, and put the bowl in to prove it. I found a nice warm spot under the dog and put the bowl in but it didn't prove anything to me. Could have been 20 degrees or 100 degrees, Jim. So I took the bowl out again.

Next I had to grease my baking tin. Now that was something I did know a little about. Out to the garage for the grease-gun. Pump-pump. Done.

Finally you told me to put the dough into the greased tin, press it down well, and bake it in a low oven for four hours. Oh, Jim, that was a tricky one to be faced with right at the end of the recipe. You see, our stove is a pretty old one and it is up on cast-iron legs; the oven is at least eight inches off the ground. But – you wanted a low oven so a low oven you had to have. It took me about twenty minutes to hacksaw off each leg, but I managed it, and in went my bread.

I will be frank with you, Jim, and confess that when I took my loaf out four hours later I was disappointed. It did not even look like a loaf. It was sort of black and blistery and it sat very low in the tin. Nor did it smell like a loaf. It smelt like an Italian garage on a hot day. And I couldn't get it out of the tin. I remember you saying to pass a knife round the edge and shake it out but the knife wouldn't go in. Eventually I drilled a hole in the crust of the loaf, inserted the end of a crowbar and, using the edge of the tin as a fulcrum, threw all my weight on the other end with the object of prising the loaf out. It sort of worked. There was a splintering noise, the crust gave way and I was flat on my back. There was no sign of the interior of the loaf.

I found the interior of the loaf the following morning. On the ceiling. A great lump of semi-cooked, rancid dough had hit the ceiling, started to droop, and then congealed into a cross between a argoyle and one of those conical plaster ceiling-fittings which electric lights used to hang from.

Far be it from me to criticise, Jim, but are you sure that your recipes aren't a wee bit complicated? I happen to be a handy, practical sort of chap, but many of your listeners are women, Jim, and how some of them would have coped . . .

Well, you said at the end of the recipe that you would like to hear how our bread has turned out so I am only too happy to oblige:

My loaf is like a weird, weird rose.

DNDNDNDNDNDNDNDNDNDN

Prevention is better than cure

Thomas Fuller
'*The Histories of the Worthies of England*'

UNTIL recently, my knowledge of Herbert Tozer, last of the literalists, was confined to a couple of indignant messages from him. 'Kindly refrain from saying "best foot forward",' he wrote after I had used the phrase in a broadcast. 'No one has more than two feet. In future, please amend to "better foot forward".' Similarly, after I'd uttered publicly the proverb 'Still waters run deep', I received a telegram from him – 'If waters are still how can they run at all question mark.'

Impressed, I showed these admonitions to Sir Jack Longland, our Chairman on that last infirmity of noble minds, the 'My Word!' quiz programme. To my surprise, Jack coloured up like a girl. Then, after some hesitation, he admitted acquaintanceship with Tozer. 'It was exactly that trick of literalism,' he said, 'which helped Herbert work his ticket out of the Army.'

It was an odd story. Tozer, a National Service conscript, had only been in Catterick Camp two days when he came to the conclusion that the Army was no kind of life for his kind of man. But how to persuade them to sever the connection? He fell back upon literalism.

When, the following morning on the parade-ground, the Sergeant Major instructed his squad to stand at ease, Herbert left the parade-ground and went absent without leave. They picked him up a week later in a South of England town. On being brought before his C.O., Herbert claimed firmly that he had only been obeying orders. 'I was told, sir, that a good soldier always obeys the last order given.'

'Your last order, Tozer,' the C.O. said coldly, 'was to stand at ease.'

'With respect, sir, that was not what the Sergeant Major said. If, sir, you would request the Sergeant Major to repeat the order exactly as he uttered it, sir?'

The C.O., a just man, nodded at the Sergeant Major. The S.M.

cleared his throat obediently. Then, in traditional manner, he bellowed –
'Squa-hod . . . Squad, stand at . . . *hayes!*'

'Exactly, sir. And Hayes is a small town in Middlesex, not far from London Airport. That was where I proceeded to go and stand, sir. As I received no orders rescinding that instruction, sir, I have been standing there these past seven days.'

They had no alternative but to acquit and release him. The Army is possibly the last bastion of literalism, particularly with respect to what it calls 'words of command'.

It was this sensitivity that Herbert continued to exploit. Ordered, a couple of days later, to 'Quick March!', he again left the parade-ground. This time he secreted himself within a large ammunition box, inside which he had taken the precaution of boring air-holes and storing ample provisions.

It was five days before they found him. Brought before the C.O., he again requested that the N.C.O. responsible for the quick-march order repeat the word of command. Grimly the C.O. motioned the N.C.O. so to do. 'Squa-hod,' bellowed the Drill Sergeant, 'Squad, quick . . . *hutch!*'

'The verb "hutch", is a sixteenth-century word,' explained Herbert. 'It means "to lay up in a hutch or chest". And the word "chest" is defined as "a large box of strong construction" – an adequate description, I would venture to say, sir, of the container to which I proceeded. And, *en passant*, sir, may I make a suggestion regarding the use of the word "quick". It is an adjective, sir. The more correct qualifier would be "quickly" . . . "Quickly hutch!"'

The C.O. had little bits of spit showing at the corners of his mouth but, stickler that he was for the niceties, he motioned to Prisoners' Escort to march Herbert away. It was when Herbert appeared before him the very next day, this time following an unconventional response to the command 'Eyes Right!', that a despatch-rider was sent to purchase a copy of *The Shorter Oxford English Dictionary*. The command to eyes-right had, as is the Army way, been vouchsafed in the form of 'Eyes . . . *hight!*' – whereupon Herbert had smartly proceeded to pull a box of mascara from his battle-dress and daub it profusely upon his eyelashes and eyelids. To the C.O.'s chagrin, the *Shorter Oxford* unequivocally confirmed that 'hight' means 'to embellish or ornament'. (Early M.E., huihten, of doubtful origin, 1633.)

The decisive battle was fought, appropriately, at Herbert Tozer's Passing Out parade. On the very first word of command – the order to come to attention – Herbert marched himself away. This time, however, he was immediately intercepted by the waiting Military Police who had been set to observe his every movement.

On the C.O.'s desk, next to his latest amended copy of Q.R.s – Queen's Regulations, for the non-military – lay the by now well-thumbed *Shorter Oxford*. 'All that happened,' snarled the C.O., 'was that the parade was called to attention. Those were the only words of command given.'

'But may I remind you of the manner of their utterance, sir?' Herbert said. 'We were told "Parade . . . *shun!*" The verb "shun", sir – and do, by all means, look it up – the verb "shun" means "avoid, eschew or seek safety by concealment from". Which I did, sir.'

'And over-reached yourself, Tozer,' the C.O. said. 'Look, lad.' The dictionary flipped open immediately to the correct page, for a bookmark had already been inserted there. 'The verb "shun" can only be used *transitively*. In other words, for it to have the meaning you gave it, there has to be an *object* after it; as in "shun drink", or "shun intellectuals". Without that "object", its only possible definition is "Diminutive of stand to attention". Which you didn't do, cockychops.' The C.O. turned to the Adjutant. 'Well done, Simon. Think we've got grounds for a court-martial?'

'If you want my opinion, sir,' the Adjutant said, 'We've got grounds for a firing-squad. Just to make sure, though, I'll send the papers off to the Education Officer, together with a copy of the appropriate Q.R. regarding punishments for desertion.'

'In that case, sir,' Herbert said, 'may I submit a defence-brief to him? Quoting some further references anent the disputed definition?'

'Submit all the anent you wish,' said the C.O., who was not without style.

You can't help feeling sorry for the man. What he had forgotten was that no literalist relies on the *Shorter Oxford*. Herbert's brief was based firmly on the thirteen-volume *Oxford*. There, with massive authority, is printed an alternative use of 'shun' – as an *intransitive* verb. Its meaning is 'Move away, go aside, fly'.

Herbert was honourably discharged from the Army within two weeks. The other factor which the C.O. had forgotten was that the Div. Educational Officer was Brigadier J. Longland. Jack's judgment on the relative merits of Herbert's argument as against the Army's was characteristically cogent:

'Brief on "shun" is better than Q.R.'

FMFMFMFMFMFMFMFMFMFM

If winter comes, can spring be far behind?

Percy Bysshe Shelley
'Ode to the West Wind'

A YEAR or so ago I had occasion to go to Moscow (a cool
sentence which tells nothing of the panic, soul-searching,
worry and frantic organising which actually took place prior
to embarkation). It fell to me, a thrusting, youngish television
executive, to see a Russian about a play.

The time of the year was February, and Moscow in February, according to a vodka-pickled ex-foreign correspondent I happened to meet
on a 14A bus, is cold enough to freeze the wheels off a brass cannon.
So off I went to Moss Bros. and hired myself a fur hat with flaps,
galoshes, ski gloves, and an enormous fur-lined overcoat. I held a dress
parade when I reached home and my wife said that I looked like a
cross between a used flue-brush and a pregnant yeti. Happily my wife
was coming with me and I was able to point out that, dressed for
the Steppes, she looked like a fur-bearing pear. But at least we
reckoned that we would be warm; poor trusting innocents that we
were.

I never did like flying and when we arrived at London Airport I had
the familiar sensation of disquiet; as though a cold potato had lodged
half-way down my gullet.

We arrived in comfortable time, as is our custom; that is to say, two
hours before we needed to. Our nerves were not helped by the broadcast announcements. Moscow is a peculiarly upsetting place to be bound
for because almost all the half-heard announcements seemed to refer
to it: 'Last call for flight 724. All passengers mus' go to . . .' 'All passengers for BOAC mus' go . . .'

A further disagreeable factor was the temperature in the Departure
Lounge. Reading outwards from my long woollen combs, I was
wearing about eight inches of heavy insulation. After five minutes I was
sweating like a carthorse.

But we arrived in Moscow safely and perhaps I can pass on a few tips and wrinkles to others preparing a similar expedition.

If you are approached on the tarmac by a photographer who asks you to stand at the top of the aircraft ladder, wave happily, and then step backwards into the aircraft, do benefit from my experience and first make sure that there is an aircraft backed onto the ladder.

Do not have a comeover when you land and find that you are at a place called 'Mockba' and scream that you've been hijacked and try to shut yourself in the loo and have to be given brandy by your wife; 'Mockba' is the way the Russians spell Moscow.

Don't expect too much from Russian plumbing. All Russian lavatory cisterns are made by the same firm and none of them works. Or rather, they overwork. Instead of the water gushing forth on demand, building up again, and then stopping, due to a small design deficiency there is no build-up and no gush on demand, just a steady, noisy trickle of water through the works night and day. So what you do is this. You take the porcelain lid off with your right hand and feel down in the water with you left hand. Somewhere at the bottom there is a rubber seating-valve thing. Press this firmly down and the trickle ceases.

Note to the above: A little way up Gorki Prospect, on the left, is a small jeweller's shop which specialises in drying out wrist-watches.

The steward on the aircraft told me always to wear my fur hat and always to wear it with the flaps down and the strings tied firmly under my chin, and I think this was very good advice. The only thing is that fur hats are very bulky things and at first I kept rolling out of bed. This can be avoided by stacking a couple of bricks on the pillow either side of the head.

I have left the Golden Tip until last, because it is very important and I had to find it out for myself.

There is a fallacy in the system of clothing you are advised to wear to combat the Russian winter. When you are standing erect the clothing is warm enough; but when you are walking, or bending down . . .

All fur-lined overcoats have a slit up the back. All jackets have a slit up the back. All winter long-johns have a slit at the back. When you bend down in Red Square there is nothing between your vitals and the east wind of Siberia but the seam in your trousers – virtually a dotted line. Your rear portion is almost totally unprotected; a sitting target for frostbite.

I gave the problem considerable thought and came up with a practical answer. You take *two* fur hats with you to Moscow. Each morning, before dressing, in the privacy of your own bedroom, you arrange two basins on two chairs. In basin A you stir a mixture of flour and water until it reaches the consistency of cream. You then take a pair of scissors and your second fur hat and snip off enough fur to fill basin B. Lowering your pyjama trousers (or raising your nightdress, as appropriate) you sit in basin A. You then walk about a bit until tacky and sit in basin B. A further turn round the room to dry off and you are fully protected for twenty-four hours against the iciest wind blowing round the Urals.

But, you are probably saying, the flaps on my long winter underwear always stays shut; and anyway, I won't be bending down.

I say, don't take chances. They can spring open with the ordinary movements of walking. So:

If winter combs can spring – befur behind.

DNDNDNDNDNDNDNDNDNDN

A crown is no cure for the headache

Benjamin Franklin
'Poor Richard's Almanack'

MY grandmother was a great one for axioms. Her favourite was, 'The unexpected doesn't always happen but when it does it generally happens when you're least expecting it.' As with everything else about my little smiling Granny, that axiom is sagacious, perceptive and, when you get right to the core of the situation, absolutely no help at all.

If you require some elaboration of that touch of bitterness, stay with me. We'll go back to the time when I was seventeen years old.

When I was seventeen, it was a very good year for small-town girls. Mainly because not one of them would have anything to do with me. This was due to the appearance I presented. At that age I was all wrists and ankles. Six foot three, a neck like Nat Jackley's, so gangling and painfully skinny that, in repose, I looked like a pair of discarded braces.

Such a configuration made me achingly shy of girls. In fact, at the time of which I speak, I still hadn't kissed any female who was not either a blood-relation or four-legged.

Then one day, a Tuesday afternoon, while Jan Berenska belted out his concert arrangement of 'Little Curly Head Upon A High Chair' direct from the Pump Room, Leamington Spa, my Mum came into my bedroom. 'Mrs Forbush is coming to tea,' she said. 'And she's bringing her daughter with her. You two can play together while we talk.'

The news did not stir me. Although I'd never seen the daughter, I had seen Mrs Forbush. About as sexy as the General Council of the TUC. So I just grunted and continued cutting out the advertisements for half-slips in *The Draper's Record*. An hour later, the door opened again and my mother pushed Lila in.

Lila. Thinking back on her, even across this arch of decades, my marrow-bone still melts. A raven-eyed, black-haired shimmer of wet-lipped ripeness. Just turned sixteen, and wearing those shiny artificial-silk stockings with the overstated seam.

'Well,' my Mum said as she left us, 'play nicely.' I remained inert, just staring at Lila. Never, in the whole of my life-span, had I ever gazed on anything so utterly – *tangible*.

She scanned me the way a decorator does a house when you've asked for an estimate to do the outside. I said, 'Would you like to look through my Meccano catalogues?'

She shook her head. The movement rippled right the way down! I could hear my own breathing. 'Tell you what,' she said, in a light, clear voice, 'let's kiss.'

It was just the one kiss. What must be said about it, though, is that it lasted twenty-three minutes. Moreover, the embouchure which Lila employed can most nearly be conveyed by the phrase 'as though eating an over-ripe pear'. My Chilprufe vest ran up my back like a window-blind.

Immediately after it, we were called downstairs for tea and Lyons Snow Cake, so that's all there ever was between Lila Forbush and me. She showed no inclination to go upstairs again after tea, spent the rest of the afternoon chatting to my Mum and Mrs Forbush, without even glancing in my direction. I sensed that she'd found me to be what educational circles now describe as an under-achiever.

Episode closed. But where does an experience like that, with a Lila like that, leave a man for the rest of his life? I am in a position to tell you. Ever afterwards, she becomes the measure against which every other woman fails. Then, as he moves towards middle-age – 'If only,' he keeps finding himself thinking. 'If only we could play it again, Sam. With me as I am now – but Lila as she was then!'

Impossible? Well, hold your horses. Cut to thirty years later. This month, in fact. Two weeks ago, if you want it to the day, at a friend's cocktail-party in the King's Road. He'd just taken over a disused telephone-box and opened it as a boutique. There I was, milling with the fashionable throng, when – suddenly, right in front of me, across a crowded room – ! Unmistakable. Those raven-eyes, the black hair, those pouting wet lips! It had happened! Life had managed to work me its jackpot – a second chance!

I bounded across that room like an antelope. Trying to control my voice, 'My dear,' I said. 'Please don't be startled, I'm not accosting you. It's just that, are you – oh, you must be, I can see it in every feature – are you Lila Forbush's daughter?'

The light, clear tones which answered me erased three decades as though they had never been. 'Up your kilt, squire.'

'No, please,' I said. 'Don't turn away, I mean no offence.'

'Well, you're giving it, aren't you.'

'Why?'

'I'm Lila Forbush's son.'

I refer you back to my grandmother's axiom. Also, and more importantly, to that assertion that axioms offer the thinking man everything except consolation.

Or, as Ben Franklyn used to walk around America snarling:

'A Gran is no cure for the heartache.'

FMFMFMFMFMFMFMFMFMFM

A rose-red city – 'half as old as time'

Rev. John William Burgon
'Petra'

HAVE been near tears many times in my crowded life but I can
only recall having actually wept but twice – once when I rounded
a bend of the road in Corsica and the unbelievable beauty of the
rock formations known as Les Calanches were bathed in the warm,
rosy glow of the late afternoon sunshine, and once when a horse
trod on my foot.

But I was near tears today, when the post brought me a birthday
card from a dear old lady in the village. She was in hospital – she had
twisted her ankle water-skiing in Hendon – and had taken the trouble
to make me a birthday card with her own hands. Just a folded piece of
simple paper, with a pressed flower pasted on the front, and a simple
legend within: 'Happy Birthday. With all the money you're making,
how about sending an old lady a gallon of gin. Mrs Tobler.'

Oh, it wasn't the words, simple and sincere though they were. It was
something about the faded flower pasted on the front. And the name
Mrs Tobler. Where had I seen that flower before?

Later on that morning, as I was cleaning my spectacles, everything
became clear.

It was twelve years ago, give or take a day. And it was to do with my
children. Jamie was then six feet tall, with an engaging smile and a lot of
blonde hair. He was eight. A quiet lad, for the past few months he had
been spending most of his spare time industriously loosening and
removing his teeth in order to save up the sixpences thereby obtained
to buy a chemistry set to make ice cream. My daughter Sally was six;
gentle, beautiful and practically toothless because Jamie was helping to
loosen her teeth in return for half her sixpences.

The children had a part of the garden for their very own, to make of
it what they would. Jamie had made a mine of his. He was down about
eight feet, prospecting for old clay pipes, coal, Roman coins, mud;
anything on which he could make an honest buck.

Sal's patch was quite different. She loved colour, and simple things, and beauty. Her little square was neatly raked and levelled and she had put little labels where she had planted things. She had planted a number of things. There was a sandal. It showed no signs of growing but nor did it seem to deteriorate; it stuck out of the ground and sort of retained its status quo. There was one asparagus which had roared up to a height of four feet and waved in the breeze like a ghostly, emaciated Christmas tree. A packet of frozen peas. In their packet. And a rose bush. Sal was very, very attached indeed to her rose bush. She had cut a clipping on a country walk and planted it and it made a brave patch of colour – mostly brown and green – but there was one small, red flower. Sal called it *Red Setter*. Because it was a dog-rose.

Now we had an actor staying with us at the time named Arthur Howard. A very nice actor indeed. The sort of actor who when you say to somebody 'We've got Arthur Howard staying with us' they say 'Oh, ARTHUR! How IS he?' But Arthur was not a gardener. Actor, yes. Gardener, no. *The Tempest* – fine. The compost – not a clue.

That afternoon we had to go out on a charity walk – well a sort of charity walk; my wife was breaking in a new pair of boots for the parish priest – and Arthur could not come with us because he had caught his ear in the egg whisk. It was one of those hand-held ones like a bow-legged ballet dancer doing an entrechat and, thinking two of the tines were touching, he whirred it round and put his ear to it . . .

So we left Arthur to look after the estate.

When we arrived back it seems that a woman – a Mrs Tizer, or Tusser, Arthur couldn't be sure – had arrived at the back door and asked whether she could buy some of my wife's herbs. My wife had her little herb garden right next to the children's patch.

Ever eager to oblige, Arthur had pulled up handfuls of this and that and sold them to the woman for a shilling.

'What did you give her?' asked my wife, a little puzzled.

'Well,' said Arthur, 'there was rosemary, chives, tarragon, and – oh yes – thyme!'

'Are you sure?' asked my wife. 'I don't remember planting thyme.'

The next thing there was a tremendous cry and Sally hurtled into the scene, tears streaming down her face. 'My rose has gone!' she sobbed. 'Somebody has stolen my lovely rose!'

And gone it had. Her single little dog-rose had vanished from the face of the earth, it seemed for ever.

But this morning it returned. Dried, pressed, and stuck to my birthday card from the old lady; twelve years later.

So a few minutes ago, when Sally looked at the card in my hand in a rather puzzled way and said 'What is that flower? It seems – sort of – familiar,' who can begrudge me a vagrant tear as I answered, 'It is a rose, dearest . . .

'A rose, *Red Setter*, Arthur sold as thyme.'

More matter with less art

William Shakespeare
'Hamlet'

EVER see a Burt Lancaster war-film called *The Train*? A dull title, but an interesting premise – a group of French civilians who risk their lives smuggling certain masterpieces of French art out of the occupied zone, so that the noble culture of La Belle France can continue to enrich the spirit of the Free World. The question the film posed was this: is the preservation of any work of art, however great, worth the sacrifice of any human life, however humble?

I found myself facing the same philosophical dilemma when my small nephew got his head jammed in the hole of a Henry Moore statue. It was during a class outing to the Tate Gallery and young Arthur had paused in front of Moore's *The Mother*. What the teacher should have remembered was that, the previous week, the same class had been on a day-trip to Brighton. There, on the Palace Pier, Arthur had posed for a comic photograph in one of those 'fat lady' cut-outs with a hole at the neck for you to stick your own face through.

To the mind of a twelve-year-old, the association of ideas must have been irresistible. Even the Gallery authorities admitted that it was a justifiable impulse, not to say endearing. It only began to take on dimensions when they found Arthur couldn't get his head out of the statue again.

'We've tried everything,' the Curator said when he visited me that evening. 'Cutting his hair, greasing his ears . . .' He gestured helplessly.

My own knowledge of modern sculpture can be evaluated from the fact that I once put down £75 deposit on a Giacometti under the impression it was an Italian sports car. So I cannot say I really appreciated the Curator's agitation. Not even when he said, 'It looks as though the only way we'll ever extricate your nephew is by smashing that statue to pieces.'

'Fair enough,' I said. 'Want the lend of a big hammer?'

He twitched. 'Henry Moore's *The Mother*,' he said, 'is one of this country's finest cultural treasures.'

'I see,' I said. 'Well, that's more than anyone could say about Arthur. Judging from his school reports, that hole is about the only "O" he'll ever get through.'

The Curator drew a shaky breath. 'Look here. Are we to demolish a masterwork just because of one idiot schoolboy?'

I stared at him. There was a cold glitter in his eye. 'I want you, as his uncle, to persuade his parents to let him . . . stay there.'

'Stone me,' I said.

'We'll do everything that can be done to ensure that he leads as normal a life as is possible under the circumstances. The Arts Council has already promised a special grant.'

'It's still not much of a future for the lad, is it,' I said. 'Oh, may be all right for the time being, but what about when he's a bit older? Girls? Marriage? You'd have your work cut out then, wouldn't you? Oh, I suppose he could manage some kind of married life, not the easiest, but what about if he has children? I mean, think of things like Speech Day? Couldn't very well turn up with a statue round his neck, could he, you know how kids are about their parents looking conspicuous.'

'It's the boy,' said the Curator, 'or the statue.'

Well, it was one of your real metaphysical posers. 'Art versus Life'. Oh, I know your Jonathan Millers and your Dr Bronowskis can bat a topic like that up and down for hours, but it was outside my range. Deepest I've ever been on a chat-show is Are Blood Sports Cruel. So I said 'Mind if I go and have a look at Arthur?'

The Tate Gallery at midnight can never be what a person would call groovy. That night, however, the sight of that enormous statue with a schoolboy's head in the middle . . . macabre. I said to the Curator, 'You could at least have altered the label. Called it *Mother And Child*.'

Young Art, I must say, was in excellent spirits, considering. 'Hallo, uncle,' he said. 'Got me head stuck.'

There was something in his tone I recognised. 'Arthur,' I said, 'you're enjoying this.'

He smiled. 'Got 'em all at it, haven't I.'

I realised what was needed. 'Arthur,' I said, 'when your parents had the wall removed between your lounge and your dining-room, do you remember what they called that?'

'Yes,' he said. 'Knocking-through.'

I brought the big hammer out of my pocket. 'That's the phrase I was looking for.'

In ten seconds he was standing at my side. 'Can we stop for a kebab on the way home?'

It was, I think, the magazine called *Studio International* which made use of the *Hamlet* quotation. They displayed two photographs – one showing the scene before Arthur was extricated, the other showing the scene afterwards. The 'before' one was captioned, 'Henry Moore's *The Mother* With Arthur Inside'. On the photo of the empty statue, the caption read:

'Moore *Mater* With Less Art'

Stand a little less between me and the sun

Diogenes to Alexander, when the latter asked
if there was anything he could do for him.

Was very interested to read in *The Times* the other day that Claude Monet's painting, *Girl walking by the river near St Cloud*, had been sold at Sotheby's for £1,000,000,000. The buyer was an American from Texas who wanted it very much to make into a drinks tray. I wasn't able to read the buyer's name because it was just below the chips and the paper had gone transparent.

I suppose it went for what these days is a largish sum because it is such an important painting; the first painting in which the great Impressionist had included a human figure. Just what induced him to break the habit of a lifetime and shove in a girl I am now able to divulge.

Monet started to paint his picture – the one he put the figure in – on the morning before the first Impressionist exhibition. This took place in Paris, in 1874, in the studio of the photographer Nadar – 35 Boulevard des Capucines, first door on the left, over the chemist's shop.

That morning all the young painters met in a café – the Café Guerbois, second on the right past the horsemeat shop – and a very excited batch of poor young painters they were, to be sure, laughing and shouting and ordering drinks.

There was Toulouse-Lautrec; he was on shorts. There was the nervous, brooding young Vincent Van Gogh, who tossed back his drink and strode off ('Young Vincent is so restless,' murmured Monet, 'ear today – gone tomorrow'). There was Sisley, Fantin-Latour, all drinking down litres of cheap beer. Only Cézanne was conspicuous by his absinthe.

But the figure of Claude Monet sat apart from the others, moodily stirring his coffee with a used tube of Chrome Yellow, and not joining in the general fun of pouring beer over each other and throwing bread at the waiter.

'What's up, Claude, *mon vieux*?' cried Alfred Sisley, flinging himself bestride the chair next to Monet and wincing a moment with agony.

'Well, you've done it all wrong, lads,' replied Monet. 'All you've painted is women. Dozens and dozens of plump birds. The public doesn't want plump birds – they're a drug on the market. I doubt if you can flog another painting of a plump bird even if you give trading stamps.'

'But,' stuttered Sisley, adjusting his chair, 'have you seen Renoir's study of the girl bathing by the river? Beautiful . . . meaningful . . .'

'Like a mauve sea-cow sitting on wet grass, old son. He'll be trundling that home on the old pram tonight, mark my words.'

'But . . . have you seen Degas' pastel of the naked woman bending over a bowl of water?'

'A flash in the pan, squire. He'll get ten francs for it, top weight, frame thrown in. No, laddie, it's the old pastoral scene they want these days; the old sun through the trees and glinting off the old water and not a body in sight. So good luck with the exhibish – I'm off to dash off a quickie along the banks of the Seine; there's a nice bend near St Cloud where the water's a dark brown colour; I've got rather a lot of brown left over from that thing I did of Rouen Cathedral . . . *allez-au'voir!*' And he was gone.

And so, on the evening of the 15 April, 1874, the young Impressionists startled Paris with their first exhibition. In no time at all the little salon was filled to bursting point with the cream of Paris.

Emile Zola was there with his lovely wife, Gorgon. The poet Baudelaire rushed about all over the place, uttering little cries and simply reeking of 'Fleurs du Mal'.

The British Ambassador, Lord Macbeth, was there with his lady wife. Lady Macbeth was visibly startled at the painting of the woman bending over the bowl and cried 'Is that a Degas I see before me?'

George Sand, the eminent lady novelist, swept in like a ship in full sail with her usual two admirers in attendance; a Chopin to starboard and a Liszt to port.

Probably the most excited person present was the Spanish consul, who stood in front of Renoir's picture of the large nude lady sitting on the turf crooning '*Gracias!* Oh, *gracias!*'

In one hour and ten minutes every picture had been sold. Not for thirty for forty francs, as the poor young artists had hoped, but for a hundred francs and more.

The Spanish consul paid two hundred francs for Renoir's nude and insisted on taking it with him. He cried, 'I just cannot leave her behind alone!'

As the evening light began to fade, Renoir took a cab to St Cloud to find his old friend Claude and tell him the good news. He soon found him, on a corner of the Seine, dabbing away at the brown bits of his picture.

'Claude!' he shouted, 'Claude, you must paint women! Put one in your picture now. This instant! We have all sold every one of our figure pictures!'

'And how much did you get for your purple sea-cow, matey, eh? Five francs? Ten?'

In answer, Renoir counted out his two hundred francs.

'Good grief!' said Claude, 'Deux song frong for embongpong?' He looked down at his painting of the river and the empty riverbank.

'Would you do something for me?' he asked, a strange look coming into his eyes.

'Of course,' replied Renoir. 'What do you want me to do?'

Claude Monet took up a great brushful of pink paint:

'Stand a little lass between me and the Seine.'

DNDNDNDNDNDNDNDNDNDN

Dressed in a little brief authority

William Shakespeare
'Hamlet'

THE outpost of Arcadia in which I live is called Golders Green. It features a Mrs Thora Tidmarsh who gives the kind of parties that could count as qualifying heats for the Olympic Yawning Team. At one of them, a piece of paper was pinned on your lapel as you came through the front door. On this paper was written an anagram and you had to promise faithfully you wouldn't help yourself to a drink until you'd worked out what word the anagram was supposed to be. My anagram was CXLNOIE.

That was eighteen months ago. Last week I met Thora Tidmarsh in the Chinese Take-Away and she said, 'I'm having another party next Saturday, you must come. Everyone's got to dress up as a famous quotation.'

'Mrs Tidmarsh,' I said, 'Oh, Mrs Tidmarsh.'

'Lexicon.' That's the word. 'Lexicon!' CXLNOIE. Look, you won't mind if I rush this a bit from now on, will you, but it's been eighteen months since I tasted alcohol.

When I got home, my wife said, 'I'm going as, you'll never guess the quotation, it came to me like Flash, I'm going as, no I won't tell you.'

I said, 'What are you going as?'

She said, 'I'm going to carry a flask of wine and a loaf of bread and a big card with the word OHTU.'

I said, 'I've got it. I bet I've got it. It's "OHTU be in England now that –".'

'It's not,' she said. 'It's "A flask of wine, a loaf of bread and thou". OHTU is the anagram.'

I said, 'But anagrams were only for the last party, this party it's – oh, you get on with it then.'

But every day from then on, she kept exclaiming things like, 'You'll

95

never guess what Mrs Thing from 74's going as. She's going to hang a convector heater on her bottom and be "O that this too, too solid flesh would melt".' Or, 'You know the lady who lives at "Done Rome In"?' (The husband claims to be a descendant of the Visigoths.) 'Well, she's embroidering the minicab company's price-rises on her blouse, so as to be "Earth has not anything to show more fare".'

People can be so creative sometimes, can't they. Me, I just gloomed about for the whole week, brain-racking. Friday night, I still hadn't an idea in my head, so I said, 'Listen, why don't I just pitch up at the back door and instead of going in, I'll hang about outside and be "Come into the garden, Maud"?'

She said, 'Where does the Maud bit fit in?'

I said, 'You're getting more like your mother every day.'

Comes Saturday night, I'm no further on. Away she went with her flask of wine and her Hovis and I said I'd join her a bit later because my mind works better under deadline conditions. After about an hour of sitting with my eyes closed, the hunger pangs struck, so I wandered into the larder ('When did you last see your larder?'). All I could find were a couple of rather pallid soft roes ('Go, lovely Roes'?), a box of Matzos ('You Matzo been a beautiful baby'?), and a – ah now! Wait a minute.

On the bottom shelf there was this bit of cheese. A large slice of Brie that we used for the mousetrap, the mice round N.W.11 being a bit sophisticated.

I took off all my clothes, stripped right down to the skin, smeared myself from head to foot with the Brie cheese, which luckily was fairly ripe, or 'Muir' as the French call it, slipped on my raincoat, then off I trotted to the party.

I was, though I say it myself, a sensation. Mainly, I think, because I went to the wrong house. There were about eight people round the table when I was ushered in, all of them in evening dress like one of those after-dinner mint adverts, and they evinced some consternation.

'Sorry,' I said. 'Mistake. Thought this was Thora Tidmarsh's place. She's giving a party and I'm a quotation.'

'Oh, quite understandable,' they said. 'Not to worry. Think nothing of it. My hacienda is yours, señor. But,' they said, 'why are you smothered all over in runny cheese?'

'Ah, that,' I said. 'Well, it's *Hamlet*, isn't it?

' "Dressed in a little Brie for Thora T".'